Praise for *The Legal Wellh.*

"Chris Keefer has done us all a favor by publishing *The Legal Wellness Kit*. Business owners have benefitted from his deep knowledge from working on both the private company side and the insurance side—as they struggle to navigate challenging legal and insurance landscapes to manage their risk exposure, they can dive into this book. In a business environment that has become increasingly complex and litigious, this book is your playbook."

> – Kathy Long Holland
> Fellow, University of Oregon, Lundquist Center
> for Entrepreneurship

"Keefer has crafted an absolute gem with this book—a legal help guide that every entrepreneur needs in their toolkit. With clear insights and practical steps, Keefer breaks down complex legal concepts into approachable language, making it possible for business owners to feel informed and empowered as they navigate a litigious business environment. This book is not only informative but also engaging, thanks to Keefer's ability to blend legal wisdom with a genuine understanding of the essential tools necessary to minimize legal risk. It's the kind of guide that gives readers confidence and clarity, helping them navigate legal terrain that might otherwise seem daunting. Highly recommended for anyone looking to safeguard and elevate their business!"

> – Todd Woelfer
> Chief Operating Officer, THOR Industries

"With a career spanning Fortune 500 to small and mid-sized companies, I've found *The Legal Wellness Kit* to be an incredibly important tool. Keefer's experience, coupled with real-life examples and suggestions, is instrumental in safeguarding the health and wellness of your company. I highly recommend this book to every senior leader and entrepreneur in business."

> – Shirley Justice
> President, Virtual Supply

"*The Legal Wellness Kit* is an enjoyable read, and Keefer's approach to the material is a big reason for that. While it's geared toward less experienced entrepreneurs and small business owners—and will certainly be a helpful resource for them—there are plenty of 'how to' items that will likewise benefit experienced business owners and executives as well!"

    – Ryan Martin
      CEO, Yakima Products

"As a former Fortune 500 executive transitioning into the entrepreneurial world, I found myself navigating a steep learning curve with little guidance. I struggled to find a comprehensive legal resource that covered all the areas I needed to get up to speed quickly. Chris Keefer's *The Legal Wellness Kit* has been a game-changer. This book is not only thorough in addressing the complexities of owning a small business but also remarkably easy to read. Thanks to Keefer's clear and accessible writing, I now feel well-equipped to handle the challenges of entrepreneurship. A heartfelt thanks to Chris Keefer for creating such an invaluable guide for entrepreneurs."

    – Pat Berges
      Managing Director, LEADING for RESULTS

"This book outlines invaluable, practical advice for both new and established business owners, presenting complex topics in a fresh, accessible way. Keefer's prescription for preventive legal care will help readers to avoid the pitfalls of an increasingly complicated business environment, ensuring that they keep more of every dollar they earn."

    – Tony Dal Ponte
      General Counsel, United Malt Group

"Keefer has done a phenomenal job capturing the importance of law in business. A must read for young entrepreneurs and business owners. I wish I had a guide of this magnitude when I began my journey, although never too late."

    – Daniel Schmidtendorff
      CEO, Communication Company

"Keefer has done a masterful job of presenting the legal basics required for all businesses in a conversational manner that both engages and informs. The book gives practical advice in a way that never makes the reader feel like they are being spoken to by a lawyer; rather, it's like advice from a very knowledgeable friend. No matter how long a business has been in existence, or how long an attorney has been practicing, *The Legal Wellness Kit* contains valuable insights and guidance with relatable examples that the reader can apply. It reminds everyone that no matter what, you always need to consider and appreciate core legal considerations."

    – Ira L. Young
      General Counsel, Children's Learning Adventure

"I wish I'd had the opportunity to read Chris Keefer's book earlier in my career, as it would have led to better decisions along the way! *The Legal Wellness Kit* covers a wide variety of foundational basics for business leaders—whether they're learning these principles for the first time or getting a valuable reminder of potential weaknesses in their own organizations. It uses great real-life examples to engage the reader, and I came away with plenty of follow-up notes of my own!"

    – Luke Pisors
      CEO, Ambrosia QSR

"With real-life examples and suggestions, *The Legal Wellness Kit* is an incredibly important tool for senior leaders and entrepreneurs alike. Keefer's experience shines through, making this book a valuable resource for both new and seasoned business owners. The engaging writing style and relatable examples make it an enjoyable read, providing readers with confidence and clarity in their legal endeavors."

    – Elizabeth Bingold
      General Counsel, Siltronic AG

THE LEGAL WELLNESS KIT

THE LEGAL WELLNESS KIT: 7 ESSENTIAL TOOLS TO SUE-PROOF
YOUR BUSINESS

Cover Designer: Bukovero, bukovero.com
Interior Formatting: Edge of Water Design, edgeofwater.com
eBook Design: Mariana Coello

ISBNs:
Paperback: 979-8-9909975-3-0
eBook: 979-8-9909975-4-7

THE LEGAL WELLNESS KIT

7 Essential Tools to Sue-Proof Your Business

Chris Keefer

Table of Contents

"You're in the great game now. And the great game is terrifying."

Tyrion Lannister, adapted from George R. R. Martin's
A Storm of Swords

"An ounce of prevention is worth a pound of cure."

Benjamin Franklin, from *Poor Richard's Almanack*

"The time to repair the roof is when the sun is shining."

John F. Kennedy

FOREWORD

The entrepreneur's journey is as exhilarating as it is unpredictable. The ability to anticipate and adapt with commitment, learning, and iteration is essential to keeping a business moving. *The Legal Wellness Kit* introduces a concept that can be as critical to success as customer discovery and business modeling: Preventive Law. As someone who has dedicated years to educating, observing, and supporting entrepreneurs, I am honored to introduce a work that aligns seamlessly with forward-thinking business practices.

Entrepreneurship thrives on inquiry and foresight. Just as a startup relies on customer discovery and iteration to find product market fit, a business's legal foundation deserves equal attention. Legal decisions are everywhere in the startup journey. From the inception of an idea to the scaling of operations, from the informal agreements to the fomal boardroom negotiations, the legal dimension is ever-present, often playing a decisive role in the success or failure of ventures.

This book does something remarkable: it demystifies the law, making it understandable and actionable for those without a legal background. Keefer's approach, likening Preventive Law to Preventive Medicine, is illuminating and pragmatic. Just as we engage in health checks and vaccinations to ward off illness, businesses must also do legal health checks to prevent ailments.

Within these pages, you'll find a comprehensive guide meticulously crafted to address relevant facets of business law that might impact your operations. From your business's foundational governance to the intricacies of contract negotiation, from ensuring compliance to the strategic management of claims and lawsuits, each section is designed to empower you with knowledge.

The narrative is enriched with real-world examples, case studies, and actionable advice, making this book not just a theoretical exploration but a practical toolkit for your business's legal health. For instance, the chapters on due diligence are not merely about avoiding pitfalls but about transforming legal scrutiny into a competitive advantage.

For those who might question the necessity of such a detailed guide, consider this: every business decision has legal implications, no matter how seemingly trivial. Hiring, contracting, expanding, or even handling customer complaints—all these actions are interwoven with legal threads. Ignoring this reality isn't an option; embracing it is the path to enduring success.

As you immerse yourself in these chapters, remember that the knowledge in these pages is your ally. It's about empowerment, giving you the confidence to navigate legal complexities with the same ease as you tackle market challenges. This book is not just about avoiding legal troubles; it's about using the law as a strategic asset to grow, innovate, and lead your industry.

Let's delve deeper into why this book is not just timely but essential for today's entrepreneur:

- **Risk Anticipation:** Just as entrepreneurs work to mitigate market and financial risk through research and planning, this book teaches how to anticipate legal risks. It's about foreseeing the legal implications of business decisions, preventing issues before they arise rather than managing them post-crisis.

- **Cost Efficiency:** Legal battles drain resources that could be advancing your business. Entrepreneurs can invest in growth rather than spending reactively by focusing on prevention. The strategies here are designed to be cost-effective, ensuring legal health without breaking the bank.

- **Strategic Advantage:** Legal savvy isn't just about compliance; it's about gaining an edge. Knowing how to navigate legal frameworks can turn potential pitfalls into strategic opportunities, giving your business a competitive advantage.

- **Scalability:** As businesses grow, so do their legal complexities. This book provides a scalable approach to legal management, ensuring that its legal foundation remains solid and adaptive as your business expands.

- **Empowerment:** Knowledge is power. This book empowers entrepreneurs to make informed decisions, reduce dependency on external legal counsel, and foster an internal culture of legal awareness by demystifying legal processes.

- **Legacy Building:** Entrepreneurs don't just build businesses; they envision legacies. A preventive legal approach ensures these legacies are successful and legally secure, ready to withstand time and scrutiny.

I recommend this book to every entrepreneur working to build a legacy by creating value for customers, employees, and owners. Let it guide you to navigating the legal complexities of business with confidence, foresight, and strategic brilliance.

On the entrepreneurial journey, where every decision can shape the future, this book is a testament to the idea that legal foresight is not just a safeguard but a cornerstone of success. Embrace the principles outlined here, and your business will not only be fortified against legal challenges but thrive amidst them.

Nathan J. Lillegard, Senior Instructor
University of Oregon, Lundquist Center for
Entrepreneurship

WHAT IS PREVENTIVE LAW?

Preventive Law shares a fundamental principle with Preventive Medicine: both aim to safeguard and enhance well-being, whether it's the health of an individual or the legal health of a business.

In medicine, the goal, as outlined by the American College of Preventive Medicine, is to "protect, promote, and maintain health and well-being and to prevent disease, disability, and death." This is why, during an annual check-up, your physician conducts a comprehensive "review of systems." They assess everything from your cardiovascular to your musculoskeletal health. This proactive approach ensures that potential health issues are caught early, allowing for a longer, healthier life.

Similarly, when you experience symptoms like an unusual cough or shortness of breath, your first step isn't to self-diagnose with Google but to consult your doctor. They might prescribe medication, recommend lifestyle changes, order tests like an x-ray or MRI, or even refer you to a specialist. This expert intervention can resolve the issue before it worsens, saving you from unnecessary stress and complications.

Preventive Law operates on the same principle. It encourages businesses to anticipate legal and business risks before they become problematic. This might involve regular legal health checks, where legal counsel reviews the business "patient's" contracts, compliance with regulations, employment practices, and potential claims by third parties to prevent potential legal "diseases" like business interruption, fines, lawsuits, or loss of insurance opportunities.

Just as a physician might recommend a change in diet or exercise to prevent future health issues, a legal advisor might suggest revising business entity organization, improving contract review practices, updating internal policies, or implementing better risk management strategies. By addressing these legal "symptoms" early, businesses can avoid costly legal battles, maintain their reputation, and ensure long-term stability.

Understanding and applying Preventive Law can be as crucial for a business's survival and success as Preventive Medicine is for personal health. Let's delve deeper into how businesses can implement these preventive measures effectively.

A DISPUTE ABOUT BEANS

Let's say you're the owner of a small regional chain of coffee shops, and are currently embroiled in a dispute with your key coffee bean supplier. Due to a recent change in your bookkeeping system, you've been late on a couple of payments. Now, your supplier demands full upfront payment and shortens your contract term from three years to four months, threatening to re-evaluate your business relationship at the end of that timeframe. They send you an amendment to the contract, warning that failure to sign means no more beans.

What's your first reaction? Perhaps pounding your keyboard or throwing your coffee mug at the wall? Or maybe spending hours online, consulting "Mr. Google, Esq." to see if this unilateral change in contract terms is even legal? That's what many business owners might do.

Suppose Mr. Google convinces you that the supplier's actions might not hold up in court and suggests you take them to court for breach of contract. What then? If you hire a litigation attorney and file a lawsuit, your supplier might immediately halt shipments, risking your business's continuity while you search for an alternative supplier, a process that could take months. Moreover, there's no guarantee of victory in court, given the complexities and unpredictability of legal disputes.

A more strategic approach would be to consult with a Preventive Lawyer. They could review the contract, assess the supplier's actions within the legal framework, and advise on how to negotiate or amend the terms without immediately resorting to litigation. This consultation might involve discussing how to minimize operational disruptions while also addressing the immediate issue with your current supplier. This proactive approach could save your business from exposure to unnecessary loss of business and legal costs.

{Sidebar} What is a Preventive Lawyer?

A Preventive Lawyer is a legal generalist, equipped with a wide-ranging experience that spans multiple practice areas. Their career often includes stints as in-house counsel for corporations, alongside years in private practice. This diverse background means they've likely negotiated commercial deals, managed litigation, and provided strategic advice across various sectors.

Their expertise extends to guiding businesses through product procurement, labor issues, and ensuring compliance with myriad regulations. They might have also worked with insurers on coverage and claims, giving them a unique perspective on risk management.

This broad experience enables Preventive Lawyers to not only identify potential legal and business risks early on but also to think proactively, several steps ahead, to recommend effective solutions. They possess a natural humility, recognizing the limits of their own knowledge, and are not hesitant to refer clients to specialists when the situation demands it.

Consider a scenario where a Preventive Lawyer helps a manufacturing company draft its supply contracts. With their comprehensive background, they can foresee potential supply chain disruptions or legal disputes, crafting agreements that preemptively address these issues, thus saving the company from future headaches.

DIAGNOSIS AND REMEDY

You make the wise choice to consult a Preventive Lawyer to diagnose your contract dispute and suggest a "treatment." Like a skilled physician, the lawyer first inquires about your "symptoms." After you recount the supplier's actions, the lawyer reviews your contract and discusses your business needs.

The lawyer assesses your willingness for litigation and its potential impacts. You learn that, given your coffee shop's size compared to the supplier, litigation could drain your resources and disrupt your supply chain, destroying your business in the process.

Moreover, the lawyer points out that your initial contract was heavily one-sided, allowing the supplier to demand upfront payments or terminate the agreement if they deemed your financial stability lacking for any reason. This meant your payment issues, regardless of explanation, justified their actions.

When asked about the contract negotiation process, you sheepishly admit to signing after only reviewing the dollars and cents figures. The lawyer then explains how certain contract clauses, often overlooked as "boilerplate," significantly disadvantage you. Worse, the contract likely means you'd lose a lawsuit, further requiring you to pay the supplier's legal fees in addition to your own.

It's a painful realization, but then again, nobody likes it when the doctor's prognosis is bleak. You tell the lawyer, "All of that is fine and good, but I still don't want to give that supplier any further business. What can I do about it?"

The Preventive Lawyer diagnoses your company with a bad case of "Supply Chain Business Continuity Breakdown Syndrome" brought on by an acute onset of "Accounts Payable Deficiency." Fortunately, the diagnosis has both short-term and long-term remedies, which the lawyer discusses with you.

The short-term remedy involves cleaning up the dispute with your current supplier:

- During the earlier question-and-answer session, you revealed that it would take approximately five months—no later than six—to identify and onboard an acceptable substitute coffee bean supplier.

- Since contract negotiation and development is a central pillar of Preventive Law (as we will discuss later), the Preventive Lawyer may immediately go to work negotiating an acceptable one-to-two-month extension on the contract amendment, which you'd be happy to sign.

The long-term remedy involves multiple prescriptions:

- Collaborating with the Preventive Lawyer to develop and implement a contract review and negotiation process, including preparing contract forms which you could deploy proactively (and which are more favorable to your company's interests).

- Working with your operations specialist (or retaining an outside operations specialist, if you don't have one) to immediately begin the onboarding process for a new supplier, and then developing an appropriate supply chain business continuity plan to prevent potential disruptions like this in the future.

- Paying better attention to your accounts payable practices, perhaps even creating a separate position for it, and hiring an A/P specialist.

In the end, by incorporating Preventive Law into your decision-making, you're able to resolve your contract dispute efficiently and effectively, avoiding the catastrophic effect of protracted litigation. Instead, you only have to plug your nose and deal with your problematic coffee bean supplier for a little longer, knowing that your business will certainly benefit in the long run from improved internal processes on multiple fronts.

MANAGING LEGAL SPEND

The coffee shop's dilemma with its supplier illustrates not just a singular business dispute but highlights a common challenge many businesses face: navigating legal complexities affordably. While my book isn't exclusively for coffee shop owners, this story exemplifies the daily assistance Preventive Lawyers provide across industries. Yet, there's a significant hurdle many encounter—the cost of legal help can be prohibitively expensive.

Years ago, while serving as in-house counsel for a global product manufacturer, I retained a large law firm to represent the company in a lawsuit involving a defective product. The lawyers weren't cheap, with the partner charging over $600 per hour and the associate charging nearly $400 per hour!

Less than a year into the lawsuit, by which time we had already spent over $75,000 in lawyer fees, my assistant forwarded the partner a brief list of questions from our insurance broker about the case to assist with upcoming insurance renewals. A week later, we received a multi-page formal report on firm letterhead followed by a $2,500 invoice for this work.

Frustrated by what I deemed to be an unnecessary report and excessive invoice, I called the partner and requested these entries be removed. I viewed them as a value-added service, reminding the partner of the amounts already paid. I also questioned the business sense of spending several hours on a formal report given its limited purpose. The partner refused to bend, defending the value of the firm's time and attempting to justify the level of compensation per the terms of our retainer agreement.

There was absolutely no concern for the value of *our* business.

In fairness, prior to joining the company, I'd been an associate with a private law firm for several years, so I was well-versed in billing hours for my work. My firm, like many other firms, had a strict rule that associates were required to bill at least 2,000 hours per year. Year-end bonuses and opportunities for advancement were largely tied to hitting this figure, so performance naturally became more inwardly focused.

When I later began managing a corporate practice, I began to see and appreciate the other side of the coin. Yes, law firms are for-profit businesses. And as with any business, a firm's need to maintain profit levels (and to establish their competitive positioning within the legal marketplace) ensures their long term viability. However, it may also come at the expense of efficiently guiding their clients' own business success.

Once I realized this, I began reaching out to other in-house colleagues and managers to determine whether they were facing similar struggles with outside law firms. I wasn't surprised by what I discovered:

- Growing concern as to whether services provided were always in the best interests of the company, and even outright distrust in some circumstances.

- Frustration with having to pay increasing hourly rates due to bloated staff size and rising overhead, especially when attempting to manage legal spend.

- Confusion as to why complex transactional and litigation matters were being handed off to inexperienced associates and paralegals for handling.

- The perception of law firms as not cost-effective for day-to-day inquiries, leading to fear of receiving large invoices for even minor requests.

It became crystal clear to me that the traditional law-firm model of billing hours was not always client-facing and business-forward in its approach.

That being said, there are quite a few nimble legal practices, not anchored by bloat and overhead, that offer specialized services and flexible fee arrangements, including practices dedicated to helping businesses minimize their exposure to risks. However, many entrepreneurs and business owners have developed a "riverboat gambling" mindset by necessity. They simply don't have the funds to deploy toward legal expenses when they are trying to ideate, protect, commercialize, and then scale their products or services.

And so, this handbook is designed to be a cost-effective way to help those entrepreneurs and business owners understand and begin to identify potential legal and business risks facing their enterprises so they can make smart business decisions about how to spend their precious capital.

To guide you through this process, we'll explore Preventive Law through seven action items:

1. **Business Formation & Governance:** Establish a robust legal foundation for your business and learn how to protect your intellectual property from the start.

2. **Contract Negotiation & Development**: Understand contractual landmines that can blindside you, and create contracts that not only protect but also advance your business interests.

3. **Compliance Policies & Training**: Stay ahead of the law with policies that ensure your business operations are always within legal bounds.

4. **Employment Practices**: Navigate employment complexities to foster a fair, productive, and legally secure workplace.

5. **Insurance**: Understand how to select and utilize insurance to mitigate risks and cover potential legal costs.

6. **Managing Claims & Lawsuits**: Learn strategies to handle disputes efficiently, reducing the impact on your business operations and finances.

7. **Due Diligence**: Gain insights into conducting thorough legal reviews when considering business or real estate acquisitions.

These chapters will offer tools and insights to not only manage but anticipate legal challenges. By the end of this book, you'll be equipped to:

- Make more informed decisions

- Enhance your business's efficiency and responsiveness

- Reduce exposure to legal risks

- Maximize insurance recoveries when needed

Dive into the next chapter to start transforming how you approach legal considerations in your business, ensuring it's not just surviving, but thriving in a complex legal landscape.

1

BUSINESS FORMATION & GOVERNANCE

Why do most new business owners form corporations, limited liability companies, or other forms of legal entities? Yes, they want to establish branding and credibility in the marketplace, of course, but the primary driver is limiting personal liability. As an entrepreneur or business owner, you need to shield yourself from being held personally responsible if something goes wrong with your business.

Imagine getting into a business dispute with a large customer over some quality issue, and they decide to go after your kid's college fund or the equity in your family home to recover perceived damages. That's exactly what you *don't* want to happen, and a business entity offers protection by separating your personal and business assets.

However, when you set up a business entity, you have a legal obligation to proactively govern that entity, from the initial documentation all the way through growth and global domination (*cue Dr. Evil laugh*). The process of governing your business entity requires following certain formalities, all of which are referred to collectively as "governance," a nice fancy word created by lawyers to simplify a very complex process. Failing to practice good governance could result in losing the protections that these legal entities provide, so you really, *really* want to get this right.

There is a whole lot that could be said about governance, and it might be difficult to wrap your head around all of it. So, to begin, we will start with eight key things you need to do to set up and operate your business entity:

1) Choose Your Business Entity

The type of business entity that you decide to form will have far-reaching implications, including tax consequences, so I recommend enlisting the help of a sophisticated business accountant early in the process. There are a lot of questions to consider:

Are you going to operate as a one-person outfit, or will you hire employees? How many owners will there be? What kind of products and services will you sell? Do you plan on operating in one state, or will you do business in multiple states (or even countries)? Do you intend to raise capital with a focus on scaling and growth? Do you plan on an initial public offering, or will you remain a private business?

By strategizing with an accountant to answer these questions, you can select the appropriate type of business entity. Options include:

- **C Corporation**:
  - → Provides the strongest protection against personal liability
  - → Suitable for businesses planning to go public or seeking venture capital
  - → Subject to double taxation (corporate tax on profits and personal tax on dividends)

- **S Corporation**:
  - → Designed to avoid the undesirable double taxation feature of C corporations
  - → Profits and losses can pass through to shareholders' personal tax returns

→ Has restrictions on ownership, such as the number of shareholders and who can be a shareholder

→ Only allows issuance of one class of stock for purposes of distributing proceeds, although shares can have different voting rights

- **Partnership**:

  → *General Partnership*, where business profits, losses, and management are all shared equally the partners, each having personal liability for business debts

  → *Limited Partnership (LP)*, involving a mix of general partners (who run the business and have personal liability) and limited partners (who are investors with liability limited to their investment amount)

  → *Limited Liability Partnership (LLP)*, where partners each have limited liability for the debts and actions of the partnership

- **Company (LLC)**:

  → Combines the pass-through taxation of a partnership or sole proprietorship with the limited liability of a corporation

  → Flexible in terms of management structure as well as taxation options (i.e., an LLC can elect to be taxed as a C corporation, S Corporation, partnership, or as a sole proprietor in the case of a single-member LLC)

- **Sole Proprietorship**:

  → Simplest form of business entity involving one owner who retains personal liability for all debts and actions of the business

→ Business income is included on the owner's personal tax return

There are other entity types which your accountant can discuss with you. Select the entity that best aligns with your long-term business plans. Be sure to discuss the ramifications of your choice with your accountant, and follow up at least annually to discuss whether your current entity form is still appropriate or whether it should be modified or even changed altogether.

Once you have decided on an appropriate entity, you need to acquire the proper formation documents, fill them out, and file them with your local secretary of state. Then you're off to the races!

2) Co-owner Considerations

As you're considering your business entity, you need to decide whether you'll be a solo owner or have co-owners. If you choose to have co-owners, consider who they will be and what percentage of the company each will receive.

Discuss with any potential co-owners what they will contribute to the venture. If one prospective owner created a product or is an inventor on a patent, they may deserve a larger ownership share. Similarly, if you or another co-owner have significant manufacturing or business contacts that could accelerate commercialization opportunities, that contribution should be factored into the ownership distribution. Or maybe one co-owner will be providing much of the needed initial funding, while the others will be primarily contributing unpaid labor or time (known as "sweat equity").

If there are two owners, be cautious of a 50/50 decsion-making split because it could lead to conflict. It's important to have a central decision-maker. For an LLC, you might limit the 50/50 split to equity and designate one person as "manager" of the LLC. There are other strategies, such as 51/49 splits, that can be advantageous, including benefits for minority-owned businesses. These should be explored with an accountant.

In the case of a corporation, decide who will serve as president, secretary, and other officers. Clearly define their roles, rights, and responsibilities in the governing agreement (we will discuss all of this in more detail later). By establishing transparency early on, you can prevent future conflicts and ensure a smoother business operation.

3) Set Up and Maintain a Separate Business Account

Once you've selected your business entity type (and given your business a great name), it's time to file your IRS Form SS-4 application to obtain your Employer Identification Number (EIN). Your EIN is required to set up a bank account for your business entity and report your business taxes, just like your Social Security Number is needed for your personal bank account and taxes. You might also need to bring a copy of the signed governing document authorizing you to open the account, so make sure to have that handy as well. More on that a little later.

Never commingle the funds from your business and personal accounts. The financial activities of your business life and personal life need to be kept separate. In other words, *never* use your business account to pay personal expenses (or vice versa) absent appropriate documentation authorizing, supporting, and then tracking each and every transaction. Otherwise, you could wind up staring down the barrel of an IRS audit, as well as opening yourself up to personal litigation exposure.

Again, this is where your business accountant can be a helpful resource. Remember, you're leveraging a business entity to protect your personal liability, so it's a bad look when your business account becomes a second piggy bank for your personal needs!

4) Adequately Capitalize Your Business

Yes, it's okay to enjoy the fruits of your labor, and that means paying yourself from the profits of your business—drawing from that separate business account we just discussed. Just make sure you keep ample funds in that business account to cover your operational expenses, or you may wind up becoming personally liable for those expenses.

Let's suppose you enter into a contract with a service provider. That provider completes the job, and you receive the benefit of their services. However, you've been a little too aggressive about paying yourself from the business profits, which creates persistently low monthly business account balances. As a result, you can't afford to pay the service provider.

They end up suing your business for payment. You assume that your personal finances are safe, but actually, the unpaid provider may be able to "pierce the veil" of your business entity and go after you individually. Why? Because you paid yourself too much and, in so doing, failed to adequately capitalize your business to cover operational expenses (such as their services).

5) Identify Your Officers and Their Roles

If you select "corporation" as your preferred business entity form, then you may be legally required to appoint at least one officer (typically a president or secretary). On the other hand, an LLC has no such officer requirements, though it's still common for owners of an LLC to be referred to as CEO or president so third parties know they are dealing with the top dog.

Either way, unless you're a very small business, it's generally a good idea to have officers in place so they can manage key functions in the business and ensure everyone stays in their respective lanes with decision-making.

Never use officer titles as some kind of awarded ceremonial title. Make sure each officer has a specific role and duties attached to their title and position. Once the positions have been established, make sure to define them, so everyone knows which lane they should be driving in.

In a larger business with a complex risk profile, it's a good idea to create more nuanced officer positions beyond the basic president, secretary, and treasurer. For example, a business that depends substantially on developing technology should consider adding a Chief Technology Officer (CTO). A product company with significant supply chain and operational issues may need a Chief Operating Officer (COO). If you're a smaller business, don't worry about these kinds of specialized officer positions—stick with the basics.

Let's look at an example of defined roles for a two-person software startup LLC. In this case, the co-owners decide that one owner, Jane Roe, will serve as CEO and Treasurer and co-owner John Doe will be the CTO and Secretary, with both having signatory authority to enter into agreements binding their new company. Jane and John are careful to define each of these roles:

- *Chief Executive Officer and President. The Chief Executive Officer and President shall initially be Jane Roe, and she shall have responsibility for implementation of the policies of the Company and for the administration of the business affairs of the Company. She may execute any contract or other instrument, including any agreement, document, or other instrument necessary or appropriate in connection with the business affairs of the Company, and shall perform such other duties as may be assigned to her.*

- *Chief Technology Officer. The Chief Technology Officer shall initially be John Doe, and he shall have responsibility for the general research and development activities of the Company, for supervision of the Company's research and development personnel, for new product development and product improvements, for overseeing the development and direction of the Company's intellectual property, and such other responsibilities as may be given to him. He may execute any contract or other instrument, including any agreement, document, or other instrument necessary or appropriate in connection with the business affairs of the Company, and shall perform such other duties as may be assigned to him.*

- **Secretary**. *The Secretary shall initially be John Doe, and he shall record all the proceedings of the meetings of the Board in books kept for that purpose. In his absence from any such meeting, a temporary secretary chosen at the meeting shall record the proceedings thereof. The Secretary shall have such other duties and powers as may be designated from time to time.*

- **Treasurer**. *The Treasurer shall initially be Jane Roe, and she shall have custody of all funds, securities, and valuable documents of the Company. The Treasurer shall have general charge of the financial affairs of the Company.*

6) Create Your Governing Documents

By now, you've selected your business entity, filed the initiating documents, obtained your EIN, set up a separate business bank account, and identified your officers and their roles. It's time to prepare the rules and guidelines that will clarify how your business is going to run, as well as the duties and obligations of the owners and officers.

If you set up an LLC, this is known as an "operating agreement" or "company agreement." The agreement needs to be signed by all of the business's owners. Units of ownership may also need to be documented in the form of official LLC membership units (or stock certificates if you're setting up a corporation).

I can't stress enough how important these governing documents are for your business, so you may want to engage a business lawyer to help you create them. This is especially true when there are multiple owners, because of the added complexity and potential conflicts. If you can't afford a lawyer to prepare them, online resources such as LegalZoom and Rocket Lawyer have suites of forms you can use as templates to get started. However, these forms are meant to be starting points, not finished documents. In other words, you need to review them to make sure the language is consistent with the understanding and agreements among the owners.

For example, let's suppose you have three owners in your new LLC, two of whom are brothers and will likely always vote together on key decisions. Your template LLC agreement might state that key company decisions are to be made by a "majority in interest" of the owners, but that means the two brothers will essentially make every decision, even if you disagree with it. Therefore, you'll want to change this to read "unanimous consent" of the owners to ensure you have appropriate say in key decisions.

These online resources should have most of the base templates you need for the various formation documents discussed in this chapter, and they can be a cost-effective way of maintaining business formalities while on a limited budget. As I said, just make sure to review them closely and, if necessary, revise the wording to ensure alignment between all owners before signing. Otherwise, these forms could create some unforeseen pitfalls which will cause problems down the road.

7) Document Important Decisions

Throughout the year (any year), your business is going to make numerous business decisions. Most of these decisions will be rather mundane, such as purchasing routine equipment, but some will be significant—and those significant decisions should always be documented.

For example, if you add or divest owners, pursue the acquisition of another business, buy or sell substantial real estate properties, or begin operations in a different state, these kinds of decisions need to be memorialized in a type of document called a "resolution." And each resolution should be signed by the owners.

These documents reflect real-time decisions being agreed upon, which means they effectively tell the story of what's transpired in your business. This, in turn, prevents other business owners from questioning you later. If you become a publicly-traded company, your business will also be legally obligated under the Sarbanes-Oxley Act (among other laws and regulations) to report in a timely manner any significant events that could materially affect your business.

8) Hold and Document Annual Meetings

Your governing rules can be found in your bylaws (if you're forming a corporation), an operating agreement (if you're forming an LLC), or in your partnership agreement. These should all contain language requiring the owners of the business to meet annually to discuss and approve the activities conducted during the year. They should also clarify where and when those meetings will take place, and the minimum number of owners who are required to attend and vote on decisions for those decisions to be considered valid. This minimum number is known as a "quorum."

There should be an air of formality at these meetings, and you need to document what happens there (in a document known as the "minutes"). During the meeting, acknowledge that a quorum is present, then discuss if any changes will be made to officers, bank accounts, or governing documents (or if everything will remain the same) for the following year.

You also need to review financial documents for accuracy, and discuss and approve the figures (assuming they're accurate). Spend some time discussing all significant and material business actions taken during the past year, and get approval for these decisions from the owners (called "ratification"), confirming that these actions should become official acts of the business.

All of this should be documented in the minutes, and the minutes should then be circulated for review, comment, and signature by the owners to avoid any potential conflicts down the road.

All documentation listed above should be included in an official record book maintained at business headquarters (or at your attorney's office) for safekeeping and quick access when needed. This record book ensures that an appropriate, ongoing, written story of the business is being told and can be referenced in the event of a dispute among the owners. It also demonstrates to any federal, state, or local authorities that the business is operating legally in the event of outside scrutiny.

By following appropriate business governance and formalities, you minimize exposure to risks, such as:

1. Personal liability when your business does something wrong

2. Claims by minority owners that majority decision-makers were not authorized to undertake certain actions

3. Claims by third parties that they should somehow gain ownership or control over the business in the event of an owner's death, divorce, or attempted assignment of interests

When you minimize these potential threats, your business stands a better chance of long-term survival and success, so you can keep selling your wonderful products and services to customers like me!

SETTING UP SEPARATE ENTITIES

Let's say you make widgets, and your widget-making business grows like crazy. After a few years, you're earning substantial revenues and dominating the widget-making industry. To spread the wealth (and minimize your own burden), you set up a few more companies in different states, which are owned primarily by your adult children and a small handful of worthy employees. Of course, you retain some ownership for yourself as well, and you're still ultimately involved for baseline pricing decisions for your widgets—even though you technically allow each company to set its own prices.

Depending on how you set up these business entities, this situation could be considered collusion among competing companies—a violation of federal and state antitrust laws, which are designed to promote fair competition and prevent monopolistic practices. This might lead to a knock on the door from the US Department of Justice (DOJ), followed by felony charges and fines potentially reaching into the millions (or even billions for very large corporations). Your competitors might also file lawsuits, claiming they were damaged by the alleged conspiracy among your "competing" companies.

Market Power: More Than Just Size

With the growth of your widget empire—effectively controlling the market—you've transcended being merely the largest player to become an entity whose actions ripple through the entire industry. This is what we call "market power," or the ability to steer the market your way because you're so dominant.

Your widget companies together may be able set prices or decide what's in vogue in the widget world. That's market power. It's not just about how big you are but how your size and control impact the entire market. If new widget makers find it nearly impossible to compete because of your presence, or if consumers are stuck with your prices because there's no real alternative, you're in the thick of antitrust territory.

Now, why should this give you pause? Because antitrust laws aren't just about stopping companies from conspiring; they're about ensuring consumers aren't left paying more for widgets just because you can dictate terms. It's about competition, innovation, and giving everyone a fair shot at the widget game.

So, how do you play this market power game right? First, don't let your companies look like they're calling all the shots in the widget arena. Make sure pricing and market strategies are grounded in market realities—not just because you can. Encourage a market where innovation and quality are the tickets to success, not just who's the biggest bully.

By understanding and respecting market power, you're not just playing it safe with the law. You're also creating an environment where your widget companies can genuinely earn their market position through excellence, not just through size or control.

To avoid this kind of competitive exposure, your family of widget-making business entities will need to demonstrate an appropriate "unity of purpose"—that is, when related companies work towards a common business goal, reducing the appearance of competition among them.

This means they shouldn't appear as separate, independent competitors in the marketplace.

Incorrect Structure

Company A (Widgets)	←———————————→	Company B (Widgets)

(Each sets its own prices independently)

This setup might seem like a smart way to distribute power and avoid putting all your eggs in one basket. But here's the catch: even though each company sets its own prices, the close ties and shared ownership could make it look like they're not really competing, but rather coordinating their moves. That's a big red flag for antitrust watchdogs who are always on the lookout for cozy arrangements that can stifle competition.

Establishing Clear Control

Instead, when setting up your widget businesses as subsidiaries, make sure there's a clear parent company overseeing the subsidiaries. This parent company should retain majority control, making high-level strategic decisions that align common goals.

By having the parent company hold the majority of voting shares— or control through other means (like board representation)—you're establishing a transparent hierarchy. Keep in mind, this isn't just about ownership percentages; it's about control over strategic decisions, especially pricing, which is often at the heart of antitrust scrutiny.

This setup demonstrates to regulators and competitors that these entities do not have the appearance of independently competing, but are instead part of a unified corporate strategy. It also simplifies internal governance, allowing for coordinated action without the risk of being mistaken for collusion.

Correct Structure

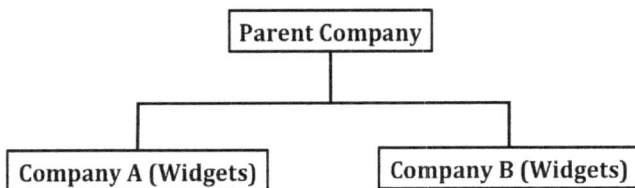

```
              ┌──────────────────┐
              │  Parent Company  │
              └──────────────────┘
                       │
          ┌────────────┴────────────┐
┌──────────────────────┐  ┌──────────────────────┐
│ Company A (Widgets)  │  │ Company B (Widgets)  │
└──────────────────────┘  └──────────────────────┘
```

(Both follow pricing set by the Parent Company)

Here's where things get safer and smarter. With a clear parent company calling the shots, there's transparency about who's making the big decisions. Each subsidiary can still have its own flavor, but the overarching strategy ensures they're moving towards a common goal without the messy appearance of collusion. This structure not only keeps you on the right side of the law but also streamlines your operations, making it clear to everyone—competitors, customers, and regulators—where the buck stops.

Each subsidiary should have its own operational guidelines that cater to specific market conditions or product lines, but make sure these guidelines align with the overarching goals set by the parent company. This balance allows subsidiaries the autonomy to innovate and respond quickly to local market needs, fostering a dynamic and responsive business environment—while also aligning with the parent's strategic objectives to maintain cohesiveness across the enterprise.

In addition to promoting operational efficiency, this approach clearly communicates to external stakeholders (including regulators) that while the subsidiaries operate with a certain degree of independence, they are fundamentally part of a coordinated corporate strategy, minimizing the risk of antitrust concerns.

At this point in the game, you'll want to meet with a seasoned business attorney to discuss things like:

- How will decisions be made across these entities?

- What's the ownership structure?

- How will pricing and market strategies be coordinated?

There are real-world consequences to the decisions you make. Remember, companies like Standard Oil or more recent tech giants have faced severe repercussions for antitrust violations, affecting their operations and market trust.

If you do find yourself in a potentially risky structure, immediately consult with your lawyer to restructure your entities if necessary. Be aware that significant changes might require government approval, especially if they could affect market competition.

By structuring your business entities with careful consideration of antitrust implications, you not only comply with the law but also protect your business from legal scrutiny and ensure its longevity in the market. Remember, the right setup from the start can save you from legal headaches down the road.

But it's not just about staying out of legal trouble; it's also about smart business strategy. Here's where establishing subsidiaries of the parent company can serve another critical function.

Shielding Risks with Subsidiaries

When you're expanding your widget empire, consider using subsidiaries to shield your empire from liability, as well as business-related exposures. Here's the lowdown on how this works:

- **Liability Protection**: Each widget-making subsidiary you set up will be its own legal entity. If one of your widget companies gets sued or runs into financial trouble, the liability stops at that subsidiary. Your other widget companies—under the parent company umbrella—remain protected because their assets are separate. Keep in mind that plaintiff's lawyers may try to add the parent company to a lawsuit to get to the deeper pocket. However, if you've been practicing good formation and governance practices, you stand a better chance of minimizing this exposure.

- **Risk Diversification**: By operating through subsidiaries, you're not putting all your widgets in one basket. If one unit faces a downturn or legal battle, it doesn't necessarily drag down the others. This structure allows your business to take risks in new markets or with innovative products without betting the whole farm.

- **Financial Management**: Subsidiaries can help manage cash flow and tax liabilities more effectively. For instance, if one subsidiary has a profitable year, it can lend money to another through intra-company loans, optimizing tax strategies across the board.

- **Operational Autonomy**: Each subsidiary can operate with a degree of independence, allowing for more agile decision-making tailored to local markets or product lines. This autonomy can lead to innovation and responsiveness that might not be possible in a more centralized structure.

- **Legal Compliance**: While subsidiaries offer liability protection, remember, they can't be mere shells. They need to operate with genuine business purpose, adhere to corporate formalities, and not be used solely to avoid legal obligations or debts.

- **Strategic Maneuverability**: In a world where market conditions can change overnight, having subsidiaries gives you the flexibility to sell off or merge units without dismantling your entire business. This structure can also make it easier to attract investors or partners for specific business units.

By structuring your widget empire with subsidiaries, you're not just playing defense against potential liabilities. You're also setting up a framework for offensive growth, where each unit can experiment, innovate, and grow without the fear of one misstep sinking the entire ship. However, always make sure you're crossing your t's and dotting your i's with legal counsel to keep this setup legitimate and beneficial.

CALL OF DUTY

When you're steering the ship of your business, every decision you make carries weight beyond the immediate profit. You're bound by what's known as a "duty of care" to your company, akin to a captain's responsibility to their vessel and crew. This means your decisions must always prioritize the business's welfare over personal gain. This principle isn't just ethical—it's a legal requirement known as your "fiduciary duty."

Now, let's talk about the "business judgment rule." Think of it as your shield in the battlefield of governance. This rule assumes that you've made your decisions in good faith, with the diligence of a careful person, and in the best interest of the company. But how do you ensure you're protected by this rule? First, practice transparency. Keep all shareholders, especially the minority ones, informed. They deserve to know about significant decisions, offering them the chance to consent or dissent. Documentation becomes your ally here—meticulous records can serve as evidence that you've acted with due care.

However, what happens when your decisions might benefit you personally? Here's where things can get dicey. If there's even a whiff of self-dealing, you might lose the presumption of good judgment. You'll then need to prove the transaction was entirely fair to the company, both in how it was decided (process) and what was decided (substance). This is what we call the "entire fairness standard." If your decisions are challenged in court, and you can't demonstrate this fairness, the consequences could range from financial penalties to the drastic measure of having your business placed under receivership, which, trust me, you want to avoid.

So, how do you navigate these complex waters? Governance might not be the most thrilling aspect of running a business, but it's undeniably crucial. It's like the rules of the road; they might seem restrictive, but they're there to prevent chaos. Keep everything in writing, from new deals to changes in business structure. These documents are not just paperwork—they're your narrative, telling the story of your company's journey and decisions.

And when you're at those crossroads, unsure of which path to take, remember tools like decision-making frameworks or even consulting with governance counsel can provide clarity. When faced with tough choices, approach them not just with questions but with proposed solutions. It shows leadership and foresight, qualities essential for anyone in the captain's chair.

In essence, your role as a business leader involves navigating through legal and ethical landscapes with the precision of a seasoned navigator. By understanding and applying these principles of duty and fairness, you're not just protecting yourself—you're charting a course for your business towards enduring success and stability.

Case Study: The Silent Majority

Several years ago, I worked with a manufacturer that was in the process of reorganizing their business structure following a handful of mergers, acquisitions, and business entity conversions. From a couple of initial phone calls, I gathered that the existing parent company had two owners: one a majority decision-making owner and the other a silent minority owner.

I requested all of the company's records since their formation over thirty years earlier. Soon, a few enormous binders arrived in the mail, full of documentation about the company's regular activity throughout the 1980s, 1990s, and early 2000s.

The books appeared to have been well-maintained by the previous lawyer. They showed agreements, resolutions, and records of annual and special meetings with accompanying minutes. All of these told a good story about what the business had been up to over the years. Documented purchases and sales of company ownership were easy to track, so I could quickly determine who owned what, and when.

However, I did find something strange in the record books. What they'd given me stopped in the early 2000s, and the final records showed that the silent minority owner at that time owned over fifty percent of the company. That didn't seem very "minority" to me. There had to be some record, agreement, or other document revealing how this person, the current majority owner, got control of the company, so I requested the rest of their record books in the years after the early 2000s.

Then I patiently waited to receive them. And I kept waiting.

Finally, when I got no response, I called the majority owner and asked her where the rest of the records were. She sheepishly admitted that the company had strayed from good record-keeping practices, but she gave me the name of the law firm who managed their business matters during the mid-2000s.

I reached out to the firm, but they could only recall working on a single transaction, which just so happened to involve the sale of ownership—a sale which resulted in the new majority owner.

"Well, there's the answer," I thought. "That's good to know." The last thing I needed was to work with a shady company.

A couple of days later, I finally received the rest of the company records, so I went through the documents and reviewed the emails between the law firm and the owners. In them, I saw a lot of discussion about the new ownership amounts, and I found attached draft agreements that everyone had approved—at least, in principle. However, oddly, none of the key agreements had been signed by anyone!

When I asked the firm about this, they confirmed that, to their knowledge, none of the agreements had *ever* been signed. Instead, the owners had simply gone about their business as usual, with the new "majority" and "minority" owners taking on their respective roles. However, technically, from a legal standpoint, the majority owner and minority owner never actually traded places.

Nothing further had been written about the story of the business, a big blank period that spanned more than ten years. The "majority" owner was, in reality, still the minority owner of the company, and during her reign, she had made numerous business decisions that were arguably not in the "minority" owner's best interests.

Finally, I had the following conversation with the "majority" owner:

> Me: "I just took a look at the record books you sent me. Did you know you may not legally be the majority owner of the company?"
>
> Owner: "What?! We signed all the ownership transfer agreements over ten years ago!"
>
> Me: "Yeah, about that … it turns out, nobody ever signed those agreements, so you're still technically the minority owner, and the minority owner is still technically the majority owner."
>
> Owner: "Oh, no. That's terrible! What should we do?"
>
> Me: "Well, since the plan was to effect this transfer, let's discuss it at the upcoming annual meeting next month. I assume you've been having annual meetings in the last ten years, right?"
>
> Owner: "Unfortunately, no."
>
> Me: "Have you discussed any business dealings at all with the other owner during the last ten years?"
>
> Owner [*growing quiet*]: "No."

Me: "So there are no authorizing resolutions, agreements, minutes of any meetings, or anything signed by him proving that he was on board with anything you've done on behalf of the company over these last ten years?"

Owner [*even quieter*]: "That's correct. This doesn't sound good."

Me: "It's not. When is the last time you spoke with the other owner?"

Owner: "Oh, about ten years ago. We send him a monthly dividend check, but that's it."

Me: "Do you think he would be willing to meet with you, so you can let him know everything the company has been doing? Then the two of you can figure out next steps."

Owner: "I'll reach out to him."

It was a mess, but fortunately, this story had a happy ending. The co-owner still lived at the same address, and he was more than happy to reconnect. The two old business partners broke bread, laughed, and shared stories over the course of a couple of days. And our noble "majority" leader, honestly and transparently, shared everything that the business had been up to over the previous decade, including all financials and key decisions made by the company, both good and bad.

The two owners discussed the old transfer of ownership agreements that had never been signed, and they agreed that new documents should be developed and signed so the transfer could take place as intended. Our intrepid "majority" owner also offered to pay her old partner an increased monthly dividend due to the growth and success of the business, which he gladly and gratefully accepted. All of this was then discussed at the annual meeting, which both owners attended.

Ultimately, the "minority" owner indicated that he was comfortable remaining silent on most decisions of the company. Consequently, updated governing agreements were developed and signed to ensure that the newly-minted majority owner had increased flexibility in her decision-making, without the need to obtain the other owner's consent for every decision.

And they all lived happily ever after.

Now, please note things don't always go so smoothly. Had the original majority owner been less cooperative or deceased, this could have spiraled into legal battles over ownership, potentially forcing a sale or liquidation under the entire fairness standard we discussed earlier.

Outcomes like these are real—they happen all the time in the business world—and they are definitely not ideal.

Your business entity *must* have internal governing documents in place from its inception, such as bylaws and operating agreements, which detail the respective rights and responsibilities of the owners. These documents should address scenarios where an owner divorces, dies, or wishes to relinquish ownership. Additionally, consider enlisting an accountant, as there might be tax implications for these changes.

Once these documents are established, ensure that every significant business action is authorized and documented promptly through company resolutions. Hold both special and annual meetings to guarantee that critical decisions are thoroughly discussed, confirmed, and memorialized in minutes. This practice will prove invaluable when unexpected situations arise, ensuring there's an accurate narrative of the business's history.

INTELLECTUAL PROPERTY PROTECTIONS

Now that you're familiar with forming and governing your business entities, let's dive into protecting what makes your business unique— your brand, products, and innovations. In a world teeming with copycats eager to shortcut their way to success by pilfering your ideas, safeguarding your intellectual property (IP) isn't just wise; it's essential.

IP protections serve as both your sword and shield against those looking to profit off your hard work. These protections include patents, trademarks, copyrights, and trade secrets, collectively known as your IP. They not only fend off imitators but also significantly boost your business's value by showcasing your unique offerings in the marketplace.

Consider Coca-Cola's legendary formula, locked away in a vault, or McDonald's distinct processes and branding. These giants have legally ensured they're the sole purveyors of their signature products, elevating their market value immensely. Imagine if another company tried selling a "Big Mac" or displayed anything resembling the Golden Arches—they'd face a legal onslaught, as humorously depicted in the film *Coming to America* with the fictional McDowell's.

In reality, approximations like store-brand colas exist, but they tread carefully to avoid legal entanglements. Even minor components of products, like those patented by Apple or Samsung, can be fiercely protected. Apple, for instance, secures thousands of patents annually, reflecting the immense value placed on innovation.

Patents, in particular, are critical assets, often discussed on platforms like *Shark Tank* where the absence of patent protection can be a deal-breaker. This is where IP law comes into play, a field so specialized that lawyers must pass an additional exam, the patent bar, to practice before the US Patent and Trademark Office (USPTO). This requirement highlights the complexity of IP law, suggesting that while I can guide you through the basics, securing an IP lawyer—ideally one with an engineering background—is crucial for navigating this terrain effectively.

However, the cost and complexity shouldn't deter you. Even if you're a small player now, protecting your IP from the start can prevent future headaches. Start with what you can afford, perhaps focusing on the most critical aspects of your business. Remember, while the process might seem daunting, understanding and utilizing IP protections can be the difference between thriving and merely surviving in competitive markets.

I will outline the different types of IP protections available to you, making these complex concepts more digestible and actionable for your business journey.

1) Patents

A **patent** represents an official declaration from the USPTO that you alone have the right to produce or sell your unique innovation. This legal monopoly lasts for a set period, typically twenty years from the filing date, provided you meet certain ongoing requirements.

There are two primary types of patents that could benefit your business, each serving different protective functions:

- **Utility Patents** are all about how your invention works. Take, for example, Nike's soccer cleats. Nike invests heavily in innovations like specific cleat patterns or material technologies that enhance performance, comfort, and durability on the field. These functional improvements can be safeguarded with a utility patent, ensuring that while others might make soccer cleats, none can replicate Nike's exact technological advancements.

- **Design Patents**, on the other hand, focus on the aesthetic appeal or the distinctive look of a product. Think of Coca-Cola's classic bottle shape. While the bottle's design doesn't alter its function of holding soda, its unique contour is instantly recognizable, adding significant brand value. Coca-Cola wisely patented this design, preventing competitors from mimicking this iconic look.

Understanding which patent fits your innovation requires some guidance. An IP lawyer can delve deeper into which protections suit your needs, but be prepared for the investment. At the time of this writing, design patent applications might run up to $5,000, while utility patents, due to their complexity, could cost between $10,000 to $20,000. Yes, it's a hefty sum, especially for smaller ventures.

However, there's a strategic workaround: **provisional patents**. These act as a one-year placeholder, giving you time to refine your invention or gather funds before committing to the full patent process. Remember, if you don't file the non-provisional application within twelve months, you lose this temporary protection.

For those whose innovations could revolutionize an industry, investing in patents is often justified. Here's a simple process overview to get you started:

1. **Innovation**: Develop your unique product or design.

2. **Research**: Check existing patents to ensure your innovation is new.

3. **Consultation**: Meet with an IP lawyer to discuss your options.

4. **Provisional Application**: Consider filing this to secure a filing date.

5. **Development and Testing**: Use the provisional period to perfect your product.

6. **Non-Provisional Application**: File within a year to convert your provisional into a full patent.

Please note, these costs and processes are estimates and subject to change, so always verify the latest information. And while this guide provides a foundation, always consult with an IP attorney for tailored advice.

Securing a patent can seem daunting, but think of it as investing in your business's future. With the right protection, your innovation not only stands out in the market but also becomes a valuable asset, potentially deterring competitors and attracting investors. As we move forward, let's explore how trademarks can further solidify your brand's identity in the marketplace.

2) Trademarks

Trademarks serve to protect brand-related elements like names, logos, and slogans, distinguishing them from the functional or design aspects covered by patents. For instance, Nike has trademarked its iconic swoosh logo, the brand name "Nike," and the slogan "Just Do It," securing exclusive rights through the USPTO. This protection lasts as long as these trademarks are actively used in commerce.

However, simply using the TM symbol next to your logo or slogan does not automatically provide robust legal protection—formal registration is necessary. Here's how you can proceed with trademark registration:

1. **Conduct a Trademark Search:** Before filing, ensure your trademark isn't already in use. This can prevent future legal issues.

2. **File an Application:** Register your trademark with the USPTO or relevant state office. The process involves some costs, typically around $2,500 for research and filing, but this can vary.

3. **Use the TM Symbol:** While your application is pending, use the TM symbol to indicate your intent to trademark.

4. **Upon Registration:** Once registered, switch to the registered trademark symbol (®). This not only signifies your legal rights but also warns others against infringement. Failing to use this symbol could be interpreted as abandoning your trademark rights.

5. **Maintain Your Trademark:** Trademarks require periodic maintenance. Ensure you renew your trademark and continue using it in commerce to keep the protection active.

Remember, while the process might seem straightforward, engaging an IP lawyer can be beneficial due to the complexities involved, including ensuring your trademark doesn't infringe on existing ones.

Your IP lawyer can further discuss with you international trademark considerations if you plan to expand globally.

This approach not only helps in safeguarding your brand's identity but also adds significant value by preventing brand dilution and ensuring your brand elements are legally yours to use exclusively. With your brand's symbols and slogans trademarked, let's turn our attention to protecting the creative works that give your brand its voice and vision through copyrights.

3) Copyrights

Copyrights are designed to protect original works of authorship, encompassing a broad range of creative expressions from literature and music to software code and artistic works. Unlike trademarks, which are concerned with brand identity, copyrights focus on the tangible expression of ideas. This protection includes the exclusive rights to reproduce, distribute, perform, display, or license the work, and to create derivative works based on the original. However, copyright does not extend to the ideas or concepts themselves, only their fixed expressions.

For example, while a recipe's list of ingredients isn't subject to copyright, the creative narrative or unique presentation in a cookbook can be. Similarly, while common musical elements like chord progressions can't be copyrighted, a distinctive composition utilizing those elements can.

Although copyright protection is automatically granted upon the creation of a work, registering with the US Copyright Office enhances your legal protections, allowing for statutory damages in infringement cases. It's advisable to use the copyright symbol (©) from the moment of creation, but remember, formal registration provides a stronger legal foundation.

The duration of copyright varies. Typically, it lasts for the life of the author plus seventy years—or in cases of works for hire or anonymous works, ninety-five years from publication or 120 years from creation, whichever is shorter.

An essential aspect of copyright law is the "fair use doctrine," which allows for the limited use of copyrighted material without permission for purposes such as criticism, comment, news reporting, teaching, scholarship, or research. However, there's a common misunderstanding that merely altering a work or using it in a new context automatically avoids infringement—in fact, copyright law also protects against *unauthorized* derivative works.

Consider what you've created that might benefit from copyright protection. Remember, while this guide provides an overview, consulting with an IP lawyer is crucial for tailored advice, especially for complex works like software or when planning international distribution.

Lastly, while there's no single "global copyright," international treaties like the Berne Convention simplify copyright protection across borders, though specifics can vary by country. Now let's explore how trade secrets can further shield your business's confidential information.

4) Trade Secrets

Transitioning from the public disclosure required for patents, trademarks, and copyrights, let's delve into the realm of **trade secrets**—those confidential business gems that gain their power from remaining under wraps. A trade secret can be any information that provides a business advantage over competitors who don't know or use it, from manufacturing processes to customer lists.

Unlike other IP, there's no government-backed registry for trade secrets; their protection lies in their secrecy. Think of Coca-Cola's legendary formula or consider Google's search algorithms—both fiercely guarded secrets.

To safeguard your trade secrets, develop stringent policies and standard operating procedures (SOPs) for information handling. Ensure all personnel with access are trained and have signed confidentiality agreements. Remember, the moment a trade secret becomes public, its value can vanish.

Implement robust cybersecurity measures, use non-disclosure agreements (NDAs) when necessary, and always be aware of the legal recourses available under laws like the Uniform Trade Secrets Act (UTSA) or the Defend Trade Secrets Act (DTSA) should your secrets be compromised.

What's your business's most valuable secret, and how are you protecting it?

Business Formation & Governance Checklist

____ Choose the type of business entity you want to form (e.g., Corporation, Limited Liability Company, Partnership, etc.) to protect your personal liability.

____ If you have co-owners, determine what percentage of the business each will receive.

____ Once you've selected your business entity type, file your IRS Form SS-4 application to obtain your Employer Identification Number (EIN).

____ Open a separate business bank account. Never commingle funds with your personal bank account.

____ Make sure to adequately capitalize your business. Don't take too much of the profits.

continued...

___ If you selected "Corporation," you will need to appoint at least one officer.

___ Prepare rules and guidelines to clarify how your business will be run.

___ Memorialize important business decisions in documents called "resolutions."

___ Schedule annual and special meetings to discuss and approve activities conducted during the year, and then memorialize those discussions and approvals in documents called "minutes."

___ When considering multiple entities, establish a formal structure where a parent company holds majority control or voting rights over subsidiaries to avoid perceptions of independent competition.

    ___ Clearly outline the decision-making process within the parent company for setting pricing and strategic direction to ensure subsidiaries follow a unified strategy.

    ___ Ensure subsidiaries have their own operational guidelines, but align these with the overarching goals defined by the parent company, maintaining a balance between autonomy and strategic unity.

    ___ Retain seasoned business counsel as you navigate these waters.

___ Protect all of your IP by securing patents, trademarks, and copyrights, and by implementing robust policies to guard trade secrets. Retain IP counsel to guide you through this process.

2

CONTRACT NEGOTIATION & DEVELOPMENT

Businesses are required to enter into agreements with everyone from purchasers and distributors to vendors and suppliers. That's just a normal part of doing business. So it's amazing how many of them lack a formalized process for reviewing, negotiating, and developing contracts. Instead, in most cases, individuals from several different departments are given free rein to sign anything that comes their way as a matter of "routine business," even if they don't fully understand how they are exposing the company to risk.

This is a dangerous game that far too many businesses play, especially small and mid-sized companies.

Let me put this in the strongest terms possible. It's absolutely imperative that you review and analyze every contract *before you sign* to make sure you identify any potential areas of concern. If necessary, you can explore opportunities for further negotiation or clarification with the other party. The legalese of even a "standard" contract can hide unrealistic liabilities or impossible performance items within the fine print, and if you don't deal with them now, before signing, they could cause you no end of headaches down the road.

Don't assume, just because certain vendors or distributors may seem friendly and reputable, that they won't create a contract that gives them an unfair advantage. It happens all the time in practically every industry. I know, because I've seen and experienced it count-less times.

Yes, negotiating, renegotiating, and developing contracts is tedious, and as a business owner, you have plenty of other things demanding your time. However, being proactive about your contracting process will ensure that you don't take on any unnecessary risks in your business relationships. It's worth the time and effort to do it right! The survival of your business may depend on it.

THE REAL WORLD OF CONTRACTS

Contracts come in all shapes and sizes and can take many different forms. For example:

- Agreements

- Licenses

- Leases

- Purchase Orders

- Terms & Conditions

- Releases

- Waivers

- Renewals

- Amendments

- Addenda

- Modifications

- IOUs

- Handshake deals

Any type of agreement that you make with another party to do, or not do, something could be considered, from a legal standpoint, a contract.

In an ideal world, a contract serves a crucial purpose: it creates predictability for both parties in a business relationship. Everything is documented, ensuring both parties know exactly what's expected of them. Expectations, along with the consequences of not meeting them, are clearly defined. With terms set in black and white and signed by both parties, the likelihood of litigation is significantly reduced. However, this scenario assumes perfection, which is rarely achieved in reality.

In the real world, predictability often gets lost in translation. The terms one party assumed would be included might be missing, misstated, or just plain confusing. Here's the rub: lawyers draft contracts primarily for their clients' benefit, not necessarily for mutual advantage. This means contracts can be laden with one-sided language, crafted to shield only their client's interests, which can lead to dire consequences if not caught and corrected before signing.

Many business owners brush off the fine print as "just boilerplate legalese," believing lawyers pad documents with it for no good reason other than to inflate their bill. Here's a little secret from the legal world: those dense, often dismissed paragraphs usually have a very specific intent. If you're not clued into what that intent is, you might find yourself blindsided down the line. Every contract provision deserves your attention, regardless of how tempting it might be to just sign and move on.

And what about legalese? It's the convoluted language that turns straightforward agreements into cryptic puzzles. For example, instead of a simple "You can't copy this," legalese might instead declare, "The party of the first part shall not replicate, duplicate, or otherwise reproduce the intellectual property of the party of the second part without express written consent, such consent not to be unreasonably withheld."

Now, to give lawyers their due, they've survived a rigorous indoctrination known as law school, where they're trained to anticipate every conceivable mishap that could befall their client, and they become proficient in this arcane dialect called legalese. By the time they're out in the world, they've transformed into these enigmatic figures, often seen as both necessary and mystifying.

So, here's the takeaway: don't just skim and sign. Read that fine print, or even better, get someone who speaks legalese fluently to review it for you. Your business's future might hinge on understanding what's truly written in that contract.

Consider the following real-world examples of actual contract language:

1) May the Force Be with You

Let's delve into the significance of the "force majeure" clause within contracts, a provision that can delay, extend, or even excuse contractual obligations due to events reasonably beyond a party's control, such as strikes, severe weather, governmental decrees, and, as we've learned, pandemics.

Historically overlooked as mere legalese, these clauses rarely received scrutiny during negotiations until the COVID-19 pandemic high-lighted their critical role in business continuity. Post-COVID, force majeure language has evolved to explicitly include "epidemics" and "pandemics," allowing for performance delays, a nuance that was not standard during the 2020 outbreak, leading to significant turmoil for businesses unaware of their contracts' implications.

Consider the pre-COVID force majeure language from three different contracts:

(**Contract #1**) *Force Majeure. If either party is unable to perform any of its obligations under the Agreement or to enjoy any of its benefits because of a natural disaster, actions, or decrees of governmental bodies not the fault of the affected party, the party who has been so affected immediately shall give notice to the other party and shall do everything commercially practical to* *resume performance as quickly as possible. Upon receipt of such notice, the Agreement shall be immediately suspended.*

(Contract #2) *Force Majeure. Except for your obligations to pay us, neither party will be liable to the other party for any failure or delay in performance caused by events beyond its reasonable control, including but not limited to, restrictions of law, regulations, orders or other governmental directive, labor disputes, acts of God, third-party mechanical or other equipment breakdowns, fire, explosions, fiber optic cable cuts, interruption or failure of telecommunication or digital transmission links, internet failures or delays, storms, or other similar events.*

(Contract #3) *Force Majeure. We shall not be responsible for liability, loss, or damage of any kind resulting from any delay in the performance of or failure to perform its responsibilities hereunder due to causes beyond our reasonable control.*

The COVID pandemic almost certainly triggered the force majeure provisions in each of these contracts, but each would have produced very different consequences.

In Contract #1, both parties could suspend performance in the event of a "natural disaster" or "actions or decrees of governmental bodies not the fault of the affected party." While the pandemic was arguably a natural disaster from a purely definitional standpoint, the governmental response (i.e., closing businesses) would likely have excused the performance of either party.

In other words, a party to this particular agreement could have pointed to this provision to stop all performance entirely, resulting in some level of business interruption or loss to the other—leaving them to cross their fingers and hope that "everything commercially practical" is being done "to resume performance as quickly as possible" during the stoppage.

In Contract #2, the clause's comprehensive list and catch-all phrase will likely cover pandemics, allowing for performance delays. However, it explicitly excludes payment obligations from this relief, ensuring financial obligations remain intact regardless of these disruptions. In other words, while one side may be able to suspend its performance, the other would still have to make their payments in a timely manner *no matter what*.

Contract #3 offers a one-sided benefit, allowing only one party to delay or forego performance due to unforeseen circumstances—such as a pandemic—potentially leaving the counterparty vulnerable without similar rights, risking claims of breach if they seek to delay their own obligations.

As you can see, the legal and practical implications of these different clauses are profound. Post-COVID negotiations now demand meticulous attention to force majeure terms in contracts.

2) The Terminator

Let's suppose you're an office cleaning contractor discussing providing your cleaning services to a large company in exchange for payment. The company forwards you a contract prior to getting started. After a quick review, you realize that the contract has been largely written in dense legalese hieroglyphics, and you don't speak the language. Not wanting to delay the work, and assuming the best, you sign the contract and return it.

A couple weeks after you start working with them, the company sends you a notice terminating the agreement and refuses to pay you for the cleaning work you've already performed on the ground that "the services were not satisfactorily performed." Livid, you call an attorney friend, who is fluent in legalese and able to read the contract. The attorney takes a look at the contract and points you to the following clause:

> *Term & Termination. This Agreement shall continue until Contractor, in Company's sole determination, has substantially completed the Services. It is further expressly understood and agreed*

that Company may terminate this Agreement at any time, whether due to breach or for convenience, by giving the Contractor ten (10) days written notice. Contractor shall be compensated for Services satisfactorily performed, in Company's sole determination, up to the date of termination.

"In plain English," the attorney says, "this means your contractual counterpart can terminate the agreement *for any reason*—and then refuse to pay you—by giving you notice claiming your services weren't satisfactory."

"But my team did a *really* good job cleaning their office," you reply. "We went above and beyond, if I do say so myself!"

"It doesn't matter how good a job you think you did," the attorney responds. "They can terminate for *any* reason whatsoever." The attorney then adds, "It's unfortunately up to their *sole* discretion as to whether or not you did good work for purposes of even having to pay you for the services you've already performed."

To your horror, you realize that the legalese hieroglyphics hid some truly devastating provisions. Your attorney friend explains that you may have recourse against the company on other legal grounds, which could be better fleshed out in a lawsuit. But you're going to spend tens of thousands of dollars litigating against them, with an uncertain outcome.

These examples aren't rare; they're cautionary tales underscoring why contract review isn't just valuable—it's vital. Remember, contracts aren't just formalities; they are roadmaps of your business relationships, complete with potential detours and dead ends. Navigate them with care.

THE CONTRACT REVIEW PROCESS

In its simplest form, the process of contract review involves thoroughly reading and understanding a contract in order to:

1. Make sure all required business terms are present (and accurate)

2. Identify and address loopholes and pitfalls to make sure you're protected once the contract is signed.

Overall, the process is designed to confirm that the contracts you enter into are fair for both parties.

As I mentioned earlier, attorneys don't usually prepare contracts for their clients with empathy for the contracting party on the other side. On the contrary, they are engaged by their clients to prepare contract forms that will protect their own interests. The contract form will likely contain a few generous servings of one-sided clauses with a cornucopia of boilerplate language written in the legalese dialect, all of which can result in a business relationship that is anything but equitable, at least on paper (literally). So here's what you can do to protect yourself from this contract "trickery":

Tip #1: Use a Standard Template

The first thing you need to do is check to see if you have a standard template form contract that can be sent to the other side. If you don't, your legal counsel can help you develop differentiated standard templates for contracts to be used in specific business settings. These forms are re-usable, can be quickly deployed, and are specifically designed to protect *your* company's interests.

Tip #2: Earmark Any Red Flags

If your business counterpart insists on using their own form, first review the contract closely yourself. Make sure the business terms are correct (e.g., length of relationship, prices, quantity, specifications, delivery) and the contract is complete, has the right names, and makes sense to you. Then earmark any problematic "landmines" (which we will discuss in the next section).

Once you've completed this initial (thorough) review, contact your legal counsel to help further identify, negotiate, and adjust those red flag provisions. Most business-forward lawyers should be able to provide cost-effective and flexible rates to ensure transparency throughout the process.

Tip #3: Use Legal Counsel to Negotiate

After signing the engagement letter with your lawyer (yes, another contract!), provide them with appropriate background information in order to adequately explain the business opportunity, question, problem, or need related to the contract review. Your lawyer will then collaborate with you to provide options for moving forward, including appropriate revisions to the contract, productive discussions with your counterpart, and ultimately, signature instructions.

Tip #4: Store Documents for Easy Access

Once you have a fully-signed copy of the contract, store it in a centralized repository for easy access so it is readily available when needed in case of a dispute or clarification down the road. Make sure to include all exhibits, attachments, and other documents that are part of the contract (e.g., terms and conditions, appendices, etc.).

Keeping your contracts centrally and conveniently accessible assists with subsequent negotiations with that same vendor or customer, so you're not reinventing the wheel when it's time for renewal. And there are certain record retention obligations with regard to contracts under law, so you don't want to accidentally dispose of them prematurely (more on that in a later chapter).

Of course, you need to monitor and perform all of your contractual obligations during the term of the contract (and pay attention to what the other side is required to do as well). Failure to carefully monitor contract requirements may expose your company to financial penalties or legal action.

Navigating contracts doesn't have to be a daunting task. By following these steps, you're not just protecting your business; you're setting the stage for fair and transparent relationships. Remember, a well-reviewed contract is your best defense and your clearest guide. Don't let the legalese intimidate you—take control, seek the right help, and ensure every handshake, digital or physical, is backed by clarity and confidence. Now, go forth, review with vigilance, and contract wisely!

Now that you're equipped with the tools to review contracts effectively, let's delve into some common contractual landmines you should watch out for. These are the sneaky clauses that can turn a seemingly good deal into a business nightmare if overlooked.

THE DIRTY BAKER'S DOZEN

What landmines should you be looking for when reviewing contracts? We'll focus on what I like to call "The Dirty Baker's Dozen." Here are thirteen problematic provisions that often lurk in the shadows of contract legalese, ready to trip up the unwary:

1. Term & Termination

2. Pricing/Quantity/Specifications

3. Unilateral Powers

4. Invoicing & Payment

5. Risk of Loss

6. Representations & Warranties

7. Audit & Inspection Rights

8. Confidentiality

9. Insurance Requirements

10. Indemnification

11. Limitation of Damages

12. Dispute Resolution

13. Governing Law & Jurisdiction

Let's take a look at each of these.

1) Term & Termination

Contracts shouldn't drag on forever, so it's crucial to have a clear end date. Watch out for sneaky renewal provisions that might lock you into an agreement longer than you'd prefer. Also, be wary of terms that are either too vague or give the other party excessive control over when to call it quits.

Consider this clause from an actual contract, eerily similar to one we've seen before:

> **Term & Termination.** *This Agreement shall continue until Contractor, in Owner's sole determination, has substantially completed the Services set forth in Exhibit A. It is further expressly understood and agreed that Owner may terminate this Agreement at any time, whether due to breach or for convenience, by giving the Contractor ten (10) days written notice. Contractor shall be compensated for Services satisfactorily performed, in Owner's sole determination, up to the date of termination.*

Let's say you operate an asphalt-paving business, and you learn about a great opportunity to make a ton of money by paving a massive parking lot at a shopping mall. The owner of the shopping mall sends you a contract, and you quickly sign it without reviewing it (after all, you don't speak legalese). You then deploy most of your team and equipment over several days to prep the site and begin the work, at significant cost to your company—not to mention, turning down other business opportunities.

Then it happens. One day, you're hand-delivered a letter from the owner of the property (the one who hired your business). The letter announces that the owner has decided to go a different direction with the paving work, so they will be terminating the agreement. Even worse, they are only going to pay you for a couple days of paving work, claiming that they were not entirely satisfied with what you've done up to that point.

As it turns out, similar to our earlier example, the language in the contract gives this owner the right of "sole determination" to decide if the work you did was satisfactory. Moreover, they can terminate the contract "whether due to breach or for convenience," which is another way of saying, "if you do anything wrong, or for any reason whatsoever." Even if the owner doesn't terminate the agreement, they can still require you to keep doing the work until they decide (again in their "sole determination") whether you have "substantially completed" the services.

That's just one risk of a "term & termination" clause. There's also the danger of automatic renewal terms. Let's suppose that you have a three-year contract in place with a product supplier (i.e., the contract expires after three years). Unbeknownst to you, the "term & termination" section includes the following: "Upon expiration of the original Term, this Agreement shall be renewed automatically for succeeding terms of three (3) years each unless either party gives written notice to the other at least six (6) months prior to the expiration of the Term or any renewal Term."

If your relationship with this supplier isn't working out, you may be blindsided late in year three with an automatic renewal of your agreement if you forget to provide written notice of non-renewal at least six months prior to the end of that year.

Fortunately, the length of a term, and the length of time required to notify of non-renewal, can be negotiated. For example, maybe you don't want a three-year term. Maybe you prefer a one-year term (if the other side will agree to it). And maybe you can try to shorten the six-month notice window to thirty days—and calendar that deadline! Re-negotiating a contract can be a lengthy and drawn-out process, so renewal provisions are not necessarily a bad thing, if they make sense for your business.

2) Pricing/Quantity/Specifications

The prices of goods and services being provided, as well as the quantities of those goods and services, should be clearly spelled out in the contract. And one side shouldn't have the ability to raise or lower prices or quantities without some check or consent from the other side.

Also, if the contract language says prices and quantities can be found in an exhibit or schedule attached to the contract, make sure that exhibit or schedule exists. If it doesn't, get it added. Otherwise, there may not be a minimum purchase guarantee if you're the seller (i.e., there's no contractual obligation on your counterpart to purchase anything from you), making the whole process a waste of time.

Here's a sentence from the "pricing" section of an actual contract:

> **Pricing**. *During the Term, Seller may increase the Prices of the Goods upon notice to Buyer for any or no reason whatsoever.*

That's rather shocking, isn't it? The seller may increase the price of goods for *any reason whatsoever!* Suppose you've budgeted funds for the purchase of goods, which has helped you project your margins over the course of the next year. Then, one afternoon, you get a phone call from the seller saying they are increasing prices due to their own increased costs at overseas factories. Now, with very little warning, the price of the product you buy from them will be increased by 25%. Even worse, the increase will begin the following day!

Can the seller do this? Certainly. According to the contract, they can increase prices for any reason. They don't even have to give you reasonable advance written notice detailing the basis for doing so. The phone call technically constitutes "notice" under the contract, which is all they need to do.

Of course, you want your suppliers to be solvent. Otherwise, you can't purchase what you need from them. So it's not unreasonable to allow some flexibility in pricing due to volatile supply chain conditions. However, you have no way to confirm if their costs have actually gone up 25%. Maybe their costs only increased by 10%, and they are simply gouging you with an extra upcharge because the contract says they can.

If a seller's costs are unstable, and you need to give them some flexibility to increase prices, make sure to negotiate language to protect your own interests. For example, consider revising the above pricing section to instead say something like this:

> **Pricing**. *During the Term: (i) Seller may reasonably increase the Prices of the Goods to the extent of its own material cost increases in manufacturing the Goods; (ii) Seller must provide at least 60 days' advance written notice to Buyer of any such increases in Prices; (iii) Seller must provide at least three (3) months of prior materials invoices, as well as any other supporting documentation and calculations proving the existence of such material cost increases; (iv) the sum of all such increases shall not exceed the dollar amount of net cost increases actually incurred by Seller; and (v) any increases in Prices will remain in place for one (1) year following the date of such increase unless otherwise agreed to in writing by the parties.*

A similar pitfall may exist in the "quantity" section as well. You may be contemplating only supplying a fixed amount of products to one of your larger customers on a monthly or annual basis. After all, you have other customers you need to service. However, tucked into the contract is a provision requiring you to supply *all* products that this large customer requires, further restricting you from supplying your products to other customers. Obviously, you wouldn't be agreeable to such a requirement or restriction, so this language would need to be revised consistent with your expectations surrounding the business relationship.

In addition to creating transparency around pricing and quantity, It's equally important to ensure that the contract clearly defines any specific product characteristics to be purchased or supplied. These "specifications" provisions should be reviewed closely to ensure they align with the original understanding of the parties, particularly if you're the one purchasing from a supplier or vendor.

Be cautious of the inclusion of "substitute products" language within these specifications clauses, as it may allow the supplier or vendor to provide equivalent materials or products if the specified ones are unavailable. If you require specific products with particular characteristics that meet industry standards, list them explicitly in the contract. This will help hold your supplier accountable and minimize opportunities for loopholes.

3) Unilateral Powers

Sometimes, a contract gives unilateral powers to one side. For instance, in our earlier example, one party was allowed to unilaterally terminate the asphalt paving service contract for any reason whatsoever. There are plenty of areas in a contract where unilateral powers may exist, and every single one of them should be identified, assessed, and balanced in order to avoid introducing unnecessary risks or an unfair imbalance of power in the business relationship.

Returning to our coffee bean dispute in the Introduction, the supplier had a contractual right to begin requiring upfront payment if, in their "sole determination," your financial stability dropped. If you were late on a couple payments, even if they were due to onboarding the new bookkeeping system, the supplier could decide that your financial stability was in doubt.

Remember, the phrase "sole determination" is much different from the phrase "reasonable determination." Requiring upfront payment due to a couple late payments may not be reasonable given these circumstances, but it doesn't matter. Because of the phrase used in the contract (that you accepted by signing), they can now require you to do so.

4) Invoicing & Payment

Check to see if the contract requires payment "upon receipt of invoice" or "within _____ days of the invoice date." This is especially important when interest and late payment penalties are included in the payment terms.

"Upon receipt of invoice" means your payment is due immediately, but what happens if you or your accounts payable department issues payments on a bi-weekly (or other) basis? And if it says "within _____ days of the invoice date," what happens if you don't receive the invoice until well after the deadline for reasons beyond your control? Or if your contractual counterpart lists the wrong date on the invoice?

To circumvent these issues, I recommend revising the contract to state that payment is due "within _____ days of *receipt* of the invoice." This adjustment provides a buffer that accounts for mailing delays or administrative errors and aligns better with standard business payment cycles. Include a timeframe that matches with your internal payment processes, ensuring that payments can be made promptly without undue haste or risk of penalties. This small change can significantly streamline financial dealings and reduce the potential for disputes over payment timing.

5) Risk of Loss

Whether you're a product purchaser or supplier, you need to pay special attention to this one. Make sure you're clear about where *specifically* the products are required to be delivered according to the contract. Risk of loss provisions are sometimes hidden in the fine print in standard vendor or customer terms, so examine them carefully as part of your contract review process. You don't want to get blindsided by the "risk of loss" to goods being shifted to you because of where that loss happens during transit.

For example, let's say you source the coffee beans for one of your best-selling coffees from a large coffee bean supplier located in Vietnam. The beans are transported to the US from across the Pacific in a shipping container that is stacked with numerous other shipping containers. However, during one shipment, a violent storm produces a massive wave that knocks all of those containers, including the one carrying your beans, to the bottom of the ocean.

Unfortunately, because of the previous late payments, you were now required to make upfront payment each shipment, so you calmly reach out to the supplier and request your money back (or at least a credit toward the next shipment). A week later, you get a response from the supplier that says you technically already owned the beans as soon as they were loaded onto the barge. Therefore, you're responsible for any risk of loss to them while in transit across the Pacific.

You're shocked. How could this be? Well, it's because there's a provision tucked away in your contract that says the risk of loss transfers from the supplier to you as soon as the beans are delivered to the port in Vietnam and loaded onto the barge. From that point on, according to the contract, you're responsible for anything that happens to those beans.

Hopefully, you insured the lost cargo. If so, you may be able to recover the losses from your insurer, including the loss of business you sustain for a period of time by not having your popular Vietnamese coffee available for customers.

Where the risk of loss transfers from supplier to customer varies, and often forms an important part of any business relationship. If you don't want to be responsible for any losses to the products before they arrive at a US-based port, then you may have to pay more money to the supplier for them to take on the additional risk. They may also require you to insure their shipment to offset this risk, resulting in even greater costs. This is an important business decision, but one you need to be aware of.

6) Representations & Warranties

It's not uncommon for a contract to require one party or the other to provide assurances that the products or services being provided comply with all applicable laws and industry standards. However, you have to be careful about one-sided or overbroad guarantees, representations, or warranties in the contract. For example, a contract may require you to guarantee 100% on-time delivery. If this is something you can't possibly guarantee, then you'll want to revise the contract language.

Let's say *you* are the coffee bean supplier now, and a national coffee shop franchise wants you to be the exclusive provider of a particular type of coffee bean for a new product offering. Hidden in the contract is a provision that says you "represent and warrant" to this large customer that your coffee beans are *sustainably sourced in accordance with the Customer's Ethical Sourcing Policy, which is incorporated into this contract and made a part hereof*." And they list a website where you can find this policy.

When you click on the link, you're shown another twenty-page document online in a small font with numerous draconian obligations you're required to undertake to ensure that your product can be considered "sustainably sourced." Congratulations, these twenty pages of additional requirements have been added to your contract! And if you don't follow them, your new customer may be able to consider you in breach and require that you implement them or lose their business. If you've already signed the contract and taken numerous steps in preparation for this business opportunity, it could mean significant disruption.

7) Audit & Inspection Rights

Publicly-held companies, due to their obligation to shareholders, must disclose certain information, whereas privately-held companies don't face such requirements. Regardless of your company's status, contracts might grant the other party extensive rights to audit your financial records or inspect your facilities regularly. If these terms feel too invasive or broad, it's wise to negotiate or significantly limit these rights.

Inspection rights are also critical when it comes to verifying the quality or specifications of products, or the workmanship of services. Here's an example from an actual contract:

> ***Inspection, Acceptance, and Rejection.*** *Seller acknowledges that Buyer may not perform incoming inspections of the Goods and waives any right to require such inspections. Buyer reserves to itself the right, without prejudice to any other rights it may have hereunder, under law, or otherwise to reject anything furnished hereunder that does not meet Buyer's requirements, in Buyer's sole determination, with respect to conformity to description and/or specifications, quality, workmanship, condition, quantity, or time and place of delivery. Buyer will have the right to reject Goods provided hereunder for up to one (1) year from delivery. Payment for any non-conforming Goods will not constitute acceptance of them, or limit or impair Buyer's right to assert any legal or equitable remedy.*

Imagine selling products under this clause. The buyer isn't required to inspect upon receipt and can reject goods up to a year later, even after payment, claiming non-conformance. This could lead to demands for refunds months after the goods have been utilized or resold, pushing you towards costly legal battles for fair compensation.

To mitigate such risks, consider revising the clause to something like:

> ***Inspection, Acceptance, and Rejection.*** *Upon receipt of the Goods by Buyer, Buyer shall promptly inspect the shipment for identifiable, apparent defects or for the apparent failure of such Goods to conform to specifications. Buyer shall notify Seller in writing within ten (10) days of the receipt of the defective or non-conforming Goods of Buyer's rejection of all or a portion of any shipment for such reason. Such notifications shall identify the alleged defect, failure, or non-conformity in reasonable detail and shall identify that portion of the shipment being rejected, respectively. If Buyer fails to give such notice of rejection within ten (10) days following the receipt of a shipment of Goods, Buyer shall be deemed to have accepted the shipment and shall be bound to pay for such Goods in accordance with this Agreement. In the event Buyer determines that certain of the Goods are defective or fail to conform to the specifications*

and has provided written notice as set forth in this Section, then Seller shall provide to Buyer, within thirty (30) days from receipt of such written notice, non-defective Goods in the quantity and of the specifications ordered by Buyer. Seller shall issue to Buyer a credit voucher in an amount equal to any freight, shipping, insurance, duties, or other delivery costs borne by Buyer in connection with the defective or non-conforming Goods.

This revision establishes a clear and reasonable timeframe for inspection and rejection, ensuring protection for both parties. It also encourages timely feedback, which can lead to internal improvements, while also setting the stage for more transparent dealings.

8) Confidentiality

During the course of your contract, you may end up providing some confidential business information to the other side. For example, if you're supplying goods, you may have certain patents, trademarks, trade secrets, formulas, customer lists, financial information, pricing schedules, and other protectible interests that could potentially be compromised without some sort of protection. Your contract may lack any such provision or requirement, or worse yet, the confidentiality requirements may be non-mutual and one-sided, only protecting the other side's information. Make sure your confidentiality interests are adequately protected.

Here's an example provision from an actual contract:

__Confidentiality__. At no time, without Seller's prior written consent, shall Buyer use or disclose any confidential information or trade secrets regarding Seller's business or operations. Upon Seller's request, Buyer shall, prior to commencing the Services, execute Seller's Non-disclosure Agreement found on Seller's website [linked here], which is incorporated into and made a part of this Agreement.

As you can see, there is mention of seller's NDA on its website, along with a link. If you're the buyer, that link will probably take you another five-page document that saddles you with a bunch of onerous requirements about how you must handle and protect seller's confidential information received during the course of the relationship. And it may extend those requirements for five years *after* the expiration or termination of the contract.

Well, you may have your own confidential information, such as financial information and distribution networks, that you need to share with the seller as part of the contractual arrangement. But where is *your* protection? The contract language requires you to protect *their* confidential information and documents, but the seller has no such obligation.

If the seller audits your confidential financial statements to determine your financial stability to pay (like in our coffee bean example), they could share that information with your competitors to drive a price war in order to get the best price. Yes, you could fight the seller in court, but that would be costly, and there's no guarantee you'd win. It would be much simpler to make any confidentiality obligations in the contract mutual.

Also, consider shortening that five-year period to something more manageable (like one or two years), at least to the extent of certain confidential information received. Having to continually manage and monitor documents from an old contractual relationship far beyond its end is difficult and potentially unreasonable. That being said, you'd want protections related to your IP to extend much longer (if not in perpetuity).

If you may share confidential information or documents before entering into an agreement, make sure you have a placeholder NDA already in place before sharing. This will safeguard any protected items your prospective counterpart could receive before a formal contract is executed. While the confidentiality provisions in the final contract will replace the initial NDA, it's important to protect yourself from the start.

9) Insurance Requirements

Hopefully, you've purchased insurance to protect your business in the event of loss. If so, you know those insurance premiums are not cheap. Even if you've purchased an appropriate level of insurance for your own business needs, the contract may require you to buy more. In fact, it may require a level of insurance that is cost-prohibitive relative to the business relationship.

Don't hesitate to push back against any burdensome or impossible insurance requirements. Negotiate something that is more reasonable before you sign.

Here's an example provision from an actual contract:

> **Insurance Requirements.** *Prior to commencing the Services, Contractor shall: (a) obtain and maintain in effect for the duration of this Agreement, at its own cost and expense, insurance as detailed in Exhibit B; (b) provide certificates evidencing such insurance to Owner in a form acceptable to Owner; and (c) name Owner as an Additional Insured under all such policies of insurance.*

Let's say you only carry a general commercial policy with $1,000,000 limits for general liability and auto liability, and workers' compensation as required by the state. Well, as it turns out, Exhibit B has a robust list of insurance coverages required, including general liability and auto liability limits of $5,000,000, errors and omissions (E&O) insurance limits of $5,000,000, cyber liability limits of $5,000,000, and pollution insurance limits of $1,000,000, among others—along with a comprehensive list of add-ons to the coverage in order to protect your contractual counterpart.

The cost of expanding your current insurance program to meet all of these contractual requirements may involve additional lines of coverage at much higher limits, as well as including your contractual counterpart as an additional insured under every one of those policies! Needless to say, could be very expensive and possibly cost-prohibitive.

In a case like that, I recommend pushing back. All of this insurance coverage is negotiable prior to signing, so determine the minimum types and amounts of coverage that will be acceptable and work with your insurance broker to determine what the premium cost will be to expand your program to the minimum required levels. From there, you'll have to make a business decision about whether or not it makes financial sense, but do it before you sign. Otherwise, you may breach the contract before the ink even dries.

10) Indemnification

Out of all the Dirty Baker's Dozen, this little guy is my favorite. How does indemnification work? Let's say your business counterpart does something wrong while performing their obligations under the contract, and an affected third party ends up suing you because of it. Your first instinct may be to tender that claim to your contractual counterpart, so that you're indemnified (i.e., compensated) for any losses incurred. But what if you discover that your contract only has one-sided indemnification language?

In other words, what if you're contractually required to pay the other side's losses for any third-party claims arising out of your wrongdoing, but the other side has no such obligation? Clearly, that's not a fair or equitable situation. Any indemnification obligations in a contract should be mutual and balanced.

Here's an example provision from an actual contract:

> **Indemnification.** *Seller hereby agrees, to the fullest extent permitted by law, to indemnify and hold Buyer, its parents, subsidiaries, affiliates, owners, directors, officers, employees, and agents harmless from and against any and all claims, liens, losses, damages, settlements, costs, charges, or other expenses or liability of every kind and character arising out of or relating to any and all claims, liens, demands, obligations, actions, proceedings, or causes of action of every kind and character arising in whole or in part out of the*

acts, errors, omissions, or negligence of the Seller, its employees, agents, or others for whose acts the Seller is responsible under this Agreement. Seller has a duty to defend Buyer in all suits, actions, or other proceedings which may be brought on any matter for which Seller may have an indemnification obligation under this Agreement. Buyer shall have the right to employ, at Seller's own expense, counsel on its own behalf and shall have the right to participate in its own defense.

Let's suppose you're a snack manufacturer who sells delicious products to a large national grocery chain. One day, you receive a letter from the chain's corporate headquarters informing you that one of their customers claims to have purchased your snack product, bit down on a large piece of plastic hidden in the box, and broke two of her teeth. She now needs dental implants, so she's filed a lawsuit against the grocery store, its parent company, and even the manager of the store personally.

Around the same time, you also receive another large mailing containing a copy of the lawsuit, because you're being sued as well, since you manufactured the product that allegedly contained the foreign object causing the injury.

According to the above contract language, since you're the "Seller" and the grocery store is the "Buyer," the store can package that entire lawsuit up, wrap it in a big red bow, and place it on your doorstep. That means you'll have to pay all of *their* attorney fees, losses, settlements, and judgments—in addition to your own. Even worse, the grocery store has the right to use their own lawyers to defend themselves in the lawsuit, which you'll be required to pay for!

If the grocery store's preferred law firm charges $600 an hour for litigation services, that could get incredibly expensive very fast. And the defense strategies deployed by these grocery-based attorneys may not necessarily align with your own product-related defense strategy, which we'll discuss in a later chapter.

Well, what's good for the goose is good for the gander! Try to include language that makes this mutual, not one-sided. As the snack manufacturer seller, you should have reciprocal indemnification from the grocery store to the extent of its own negligence or breach of the agreement.

You can revise the above contract provision to the following:

> **Indemnification.** *Each party (each an "Indemnifying Party") hereby agrees, to the fullest extent permitted by law, to indemnify and hold the other party, its parents, subsidiaries, affiliates, owners, directors, officers, employees, and agents (collectively, the "Indemnified Parties") harmless from and against any and all claims, liens, losses, damages, settlements, costs, charges, or other expenses or liability of every kind and character arising out of or relating to any and all claims, liens, demands, obligations, actions, proceedings, or causes of action of every kind and character arising in whole or in part out of the acts, errors, omissions, or negligence of the Indemnifying Party, its employees, agents, or others for whose acts the Indemnifying Party is responsible under this Agreement. Indemnifying Party has a duty to defend Indemnified Parties in all suits, actions, or other proceedings which may be brought on any matter for which Indemnifying Party may have an indemnification obligation under this Agreement. Indemnified Parties shall have the right to employ, at Indemnifying Party's own expense, counsel on their own behalf and shall have the right to participate in their own defense.*

11) Limitation of Damages

If you purchase products from a supplier under an ongoing contract for resale to your customers, and those products somehow fail or are otherwise compromised, your customers may seek recourse against you. Or they may stop doing business with you altogether. You may have claims against the supplier under the contract for at least some of these losses. However, limitation of damages language in the contract may cap the supplier's overall exposure at a nominal sum that doesn't come anywhere close to compensating you for such losses.

Consider this example provision from an actual contract:

Limitation of Liability. To the maximum extent permitted by applicable law: (a) in no event shall Seller or its parents, subsidiaries, affiliates, owners, directors, officers, employees, or agents have any liability, contingent or otherwise, for any indirect, special, incidental, consequential, punitive, statutory, or exemplary damages in any way arising out of or relating to this Agreement, or the performance of its obligations hereunder, including lost profits, loss of goodwill, work stoppage, equipment failure or malfunction, loss of data, property damage, or any other damages or losses, even if a party has been advised of the possibility thereof, and regardless of the legal or equitable theory (contract, tort,[1] statute, indemnity or otherwise) upon which any such liability is based; and (b) the aggregate liability of Seller and its parents, subsidiaries, affiliates, owners, directors, officers, employees, and agents, and the sole remedy available to Buyer arising out of or relating to this Agreement, shall be limited to termination of this Agreement and damages not to exceed any payments due and not previously paid to Seller in accordance with this Agreement.

A limitation like this one could leave you significantly exposed if your contractual counterpart breaches the agreement, resulting in a massive loss to your business.

Let's say you're the buyer, and the seller has breached the contract, resulting in $1,000,000 in lost profits, business opportunities, and goodwill to you since your own customers will have to buy their products somewhere else. These lost business opportunities and goodwill would be specifically excluded under subpart (a) above, since they would constitute "indirect, special, incidental, consequential damages" (and are explicitly excluded as "lost profits" and "loss of goodwill"). Therefore, the only recovery you'd have against the seller would be to terminate the agreement and recover any sums previously paid to the seller, which may only be a small fraction of your overall losses arising from the breach.

---

1   A "tort" is a civil wrong, other than a breach of contract, that causes harm or injury to another person or their property.

Identify and try to negotiate all such limitations in your contract before signing (and certainly before any claims materialize), but be aware most sellers and suppliers won't budge on damages limitation provisions like this. They may have thousands of buyers, so letting every one of those buyers contract for unlimited damages opportunities would be like opening Pandora's box for them. However, you might be able to make the limitation of damages language mutual. That way you limit any damages exposure to yourself that would arise from your own breach.

You might further exclude from this limitation really bad behavior, such as gross negligence, willful misconduct, recklessness, fraud, or a violation of applicable law. And you might exclude indemnification rights from any caps to ensure they are not potentially compromised.

The negotiated section could read something like this:

> *__Limitation of Liability__. To the maximum extent permitted by applicable law: (a) in no event shall either Party or its parents, subsidiaries, affiliates, owners, directors, officers, employees, or agents have any liability, contingent or otherwise, for any indirect, special, incidental, consequential, punitive, statutory, or exemplary damages in any way arising out of or relating to this Agreement, or the performance of its obligations hereunder, including lost profits, loss of goodwill, work stoppage, equipment failure or malfunction, loss of data, property damage, or any other damages or losses, even if a party has been advised of the possibility thereof, and regardless of the legal or equitable theory (contract, tort, statute, indemnity or otherwise) upon which any such liability is based; and (b) the aggregate liability of each Party and its parents, subsidiaries, affiliates, owners, directors, officers, employees, and agents, and the sole remedy available to such party arising out of or relating to this Agreement, except to the extent of their gross negligence, recklessness, fraud, willful misconduct, or violation of applicable law, and further to the extent of any indemnification obligations under this Agreement, shall be limited to termination of this Agreement and*

direct damages incurred by the non-defaulting party in accordance with this Agreement.

12) Dispute Resolution

Some contracts, particularly in the construction arena, will include protracted and drawn-out dispute resolution processes. For example, in many construction contracts, there is a requirement that, in the event of a dispute, both parties have some period of time (often thirty days) to come together and informally discuss resolving that dispute. In the event that fails, they will then submit the dispute to a third-party mediator, who will attempt to bring the parties together to facilitate a settlement.

In the event mediation fails, the parties could then choose to resolve their dispute via litigation or arbitration. The former involves filing a lawsuit in a court of law, in which case a judge (who may or may not be sophisticated in the particular industry) will decide who wins as a matter of law. Arbitration, on the other hand, is a process where the parties agree on a third-party arbitrator who is typically an attorney or former judge with a specialty in that industry, and who may better understand the nuanced issues at hand. The process of arbitration would proceed similarly to a lawsuit, with witnesses and testimony, but not in a formal court setting.

An arbitrator has a lot of flexibility to act based on respective fairness issues to either side (sort of like the Old Testament story of King Solomon and "splitting the baby"), while a judge is more likely to issue a "winner take all" ruling that applies statutes and caselaw as precedent. This makes arbitration favorable in some, but not all, settings, so consider this carefully from a business perspective.

13) Governing Law & Jurisdiction

When entering a contract, the aim isn't to end up in court or arbitration, but disputes do occur, and where they're resolved can significantly affect the outcome. A contract might stipulate that any legal action must be initiated in a jurisdiction far from your base, potentially under laws less favorable to your case.

Here's an example from an actual contract:

> **Governing Law & Jurisdiction.** *This Agreement will be governed by the laws of the State where Seller is incorporated, disregarding its conflict of law principles. All disputes shall be resolved in the courts of the County and State where Seller is incorporated. Seller is entitled to recover all costs, expenses, and legal fees from Buyer for enforcing this Agreement.*

Imagine you're the buyer in this scenario, and the seller accuses you of breach. Despite your disagreement, you're now facing a lawsuit in a distant state. Typically, each party should bear their own legal costs (known as the "American Rule"), unless the contract specifies otherwise. However, this clause unfairly shifts all legal costs to the buyer, regardless of the dispute's outcome.

Many states have moved to invalidate such one-sided fee provisions, but the effectiveness of this depends on the governing law specified in the contract. If the seller's state allows such provisions, you're at a disadvantage, both geographically and legally.

To address this, you might negotiate for:

> **Governing Law & Jurisdiction.** *This Agreement is governed by the laws of the State where Seller is incorporated. Any dispute shall be resolved in the courts of the County and State where Seller is incorporated. The prevailing party in any legal action shall be entitled to recover all costs, expenses, and legal fees from the non-prevailing party.*

This revision makes the fee-shifting mutual, ensuring that the party who wins the dispute can recover costs, which is fairer than the one-sided original clause. If mutual fee-shifting isn't acceptable, you might push for each party to bear their own costs, aligning with the American Rule.

Such an adjustment reflects a business decision. If you're confident in your compliance with the contract terms, a fee-shifting clause might be beneficial, especially when potential legal costs could deter enforcing your rights. However, if the costs of litigation could outweigh the dispute's value, it might be more strategic to remove the fee-shifting provision altogether.

A CONTRACT CAUTIONARY TALE

We were engaged by a national product manufacturing company that worked with numerous vendors and materials suppliers. Over the course of many years, the company's contracting work had been delegated so many times that at least twenty managers across several departments were responsible for reviewing and signing contracts.

There was no centralized process for vetting potential business partners to check for red flags. There were also no "pro-company" form contracts in place, other than basic NDAs. This meant the company had been simply reacting to one-sided contracts provided by business counterparts, many of which were in complex transactional settings.

All of these disparate managers were signing contracts with multiple business partners, across multiple business functions—without fully understanding who they were contracting with, or the liabilities and obligations being undertaken.

They didn't understand the legalese pitfalls contained in many one-sided agreements, had never been introduced to the Dirty Baker's Dozen, and therefore didn't know what to negotiate. And, quite frankly, they resented being dragged away from their production schedules to tend to eye-glazing tasks like reviewing contract language.

Ultimately, this led to the following problems for the company:

- They assumed many onerous obligations, such as implementing impossible or impractical compliance programs, aggressive payment and credit-worthiness requirements, unreasonable inspection and acceptance periods, and overbroad and one-sided indemnification language.

- They had to deal with many vague and one-sided contract termination provisions that gave their business counterparts broad rights to terminate contracts for any reason, and at any time, without consequence.

- They were subject to overbroad and ambiguous service provisions that resulted in projects continuing for much longer than what they had initially anticipated (or desired).

- They could only claim limited recovery in the event of a breach of contract, including the inability to recover attorney's fees when litigation became necessary, as well as being forced to litigate in unfavorable venues far away.

- Business counterparts with significant safety histories and a lack of appropriate insurance were given access to the company premises to perform maintenance and repairs on heavy industrial equipment.

On more than one occasion, key suppliers availed themselves of their one-sided contract provisions—resulting in substantial business interruption and legal costs to the company.

Clearly, the company's executive management didn't understand the benefits of being proactive with contract negotiation, because they continued to find themselves reacting to problems that could have been avoided.

Fixing the Mess

We collaborated with the company to help them become more proactive in reviewing and negotiating contracts. First, we drastically reduced the number of managers and departments involved by centralizing the contract review process with a newly-developed procurement department. The director of this department was more than happy to have expanded control over enterprise-wide contracts due to the messy state of affairs.

We then collaborated with the new director to develop pre-qualification standards based on different vendor and supplier settings. More specifically, depending on the type of engagement being contemplated by the company, a prospective business counterpart would have to provide certain information and documentation before even being considered, such as:

- **Company Profile & Background**

  → Company name, address, and contact information

  → History and background of the business

  → Ownership structure and key management personnel

- **Financial Stability**

  → Financial statements (balance sheet, income statement, cash flow statement) for prior two years

  → Credit references or ratings

  → Bank details and references

- **Legal & Compliance Information**

  → Business registration and licenses

  → Compliance with local and international laws

→ Litigation history and any ongoing legal issues

→ Certifications involving relevant industry-specific standards.

- **Product or Service Information:**

  → Detailed description of products or services offered

  → Quality assurance processes

  → Samples or case studies of previous work

- **Health, Safety & Environmental (HSE) Standards**

  → HSE policy and track record

  → Accident records and safety measures in place

  → Environmental impact assessments and sustainability practices

- **Operational Capacity & Capabilities:**

  → Production capacity or service capabilities

  → Supply chain management practices

  → Technology and equipment utilized

  → Scalability of operations

- **References**

  → Client references or testimonials

  → History of past contracts similar in scope or nature

- **Insurance**

  → Types and levels of insurance coverage

- **Ethical Standards & Corporate Social Responsibility (CSR)**

  → Code of conduct or ethics policy

  → CSR initiatives or reports

  → Labor practices (e.g., policies against child labor, forced labor, etc.)

- **IT & Data Security**

  → Data protection policies (compliance with GDPR or similar regulations)

  → Cybersecurity measures and history of breaches, if any

- **Performance Metrics:**

  → Key performance indicators (KPIs) they adhere to

  → Historical performance data regarding delivery times, quality issues, etc.

- **Contingency & Risk Management**

  → Disaster recovery plans

  → Business continuity plans

- **Subcontractors**

  → Information on any subcontractors they use, including their pre-qualification process

- **Cultural Fit**

  → Company values and culture to ensure alignment with your organization's ethos

Collecting this information and documentation enabled the company to better assess whether a specific vendor or supplier would be able to meet its contractual obligations, deliver quality products or services, adhere to regulatory requirements, and align with the ethical and operational standards of the company.

Of course, the scope and depth of information and documentation required may vary depending on the particular industry involved, types of products or services being sourced, size of the contract, and strategic importance of those products or services to your business.

Next, we implemented the Contract Review Process discussed earlier, further developing a set of "pro-company" standard contract forms that could be tailored across multiple business functions and deployed proactively. We knew that some business counterparts would demand their own forms be used. When this occurred, the director would request a copy of the contract as a Word document or another editable format for review.

By the way, any reasonable business counterpart should expect you to want an editable copy of a contract to redline when they demand to use their own one-sided form. If they refuse to provide it, this may be a red flag, and you might want to consider other business partners. After all, if they are going to be this difficult in the initial negotiation stages, just imagine how problematic they'll become if there are any issues with regard to contract performance.

It's Game Time

After developing a standard process and forms for the manufacturing company, we collaborated with the director to get executive management up to speed on everything taking place. Given the prior contracting problems the company had faced over several years, it was an easy sell. We also began implementing an informational process to ensure enterprise-wide understanding and appreciation of what we were doing and why we were doing it.

Our Preventive Law team continued to get involved as needed, particularly when:

- The director or contracting counterpart had questions about whether certain pre-qualification requirements could be limited or waived under a given set of circumstances.

- We had deployed our form contract, but the other side responded with substantive redlines requiring review and evaluation.

- The other side demanded that their own one-sided form be utilized, requiring review and redlines on our side to balance things out.

- Assistance was needed to develop negotiation strategies in order to arrive at acceptable contract language after several rounds of back-and-forth redlining, with both parties digging in their respective feet.

Following implementation, the company noticed immediate results:

- Managers were no longer burdened with contract review tasks and were able to focus energy on managing their teams and making good products.

- There was enterprise-wide consistency around the contracting process.

- Contracts with business counterparts were more balanced between the parties, and when the other side signed the pro-company form without negotiating it (ignoring the "boilerplate legalese"), terms were even more favorable to the company.

- Since the contract language had been discussed and negotiated in advance, issues with vague, ambiguous, and overbroad provisions were minimized.

- The company was able to perform effective gatekeeping early on to determine which business counterparts should be considered long-term fits for sustainable success, and which ones shouldn't.

- The contracting process finally supported the making and selling of product, instead of hindering it.

- In some instances, insurance premiums *decreased* since certain business risks were no longer being assumed by the company, but were instead contractually transferred to their counterpart.

Look, contract negotiation and development may not be the sexiest part of running a business, but It's a critical component and shouldn't be dismissed. In fact, being proactive on this front can minimize catastrophic business and litigation exposure, as this next case study will demonstrate.

Case Study: Mortal Contract

Several years ago, I represented a commercial development company and its owner that had been sued by a large manufacturer. The relationship had begun a few years earlier when the manufacturer approached my clients as they were promoting a project that was going to be the first of a series of projects using a novel type of construction.

The parties entered into a series of agreements in which the manufacturer agreed to produce all of the components needed for this project, as well as obtain the necessary drawings, permits, and approvals at the initial site. The manufacturer was also financing my clients' own costs on the project, so there were additional loan agreements and a personal guaranty in play.

Unfortunately, my clients had failed to negotiate all of these very one-sided agreements in advance. As a result, the manufacturer made liberal interpretations of their own obligations regarding the timing of the manufacturing of components, including when they needed to provide those pesky architectural drawings and obtain permits and approvals. As you might imagine, this resulted in significant and wholly unnecessary delays and additional costs for my clients.

As a result of these persistent delays, the municipality eventually refused to issue the necessary permits and approvals for the project. The manufacturer then decided they would take over and complete construction of the project on their own, pointing to vague language in the development agreement regarding project delays.

In other words, the manufacturer claimed they could terminate the construction agreement due to the municipality refusing to issue permits and approvals—*even though they had directly caused those delays!*

But they weren't done yet.

The manufacturer then demanded that my clients pay the full outstanding loan balance by the deadline under the one-side loan agreements and personal guaranty. Naturally, my clients refused to do so given the circumstances, so the manufacturer proceeded to file an eight-figure lawsuit against them.

Unfortunately, the agreements had also been drafted with one-sided attorney's fee provisions, and we were in a jurisdiction that allowed them. This meant my clients not only had to pay their own attorney's fees to defend against the lawsuit, but they also had to pay the fees incurred by the manufacturer. And the manufacturer hired a national firm to represent their interests, with the lead partner charging over $650 an hour!

Litigation proved to be an uphill battle, all because my clients had failed to negotiate agreements before signing. The manufacturer was particularly stubborn during the litigation proceedings, refusing to back off their extremely aggressive interpretation of the agreements.

All attempts at settling the case, including multiple mediation attempts, were futile because the manufacturer refused to settle for anything less than the full outstanding balance plus all of the attorney fees that continued to accrue during the lawsuit. Ultimately, my clients' only course was to roll the dice and "bet the company" at trial.

After initial pleadings (followed by some motions and hearings), comprehensive discovery (with many more motions and hearings), and then trial and final appeal (and of course, more motions and hearings), the combined attorneys' fees and costs became astronomical. And sadly, my clients lost the case at trial, which meant they had to pay all of those fees and costs, in addition to the massive judgment leveled against them.

In the end, my clients were forced to file for bankruptcy.

Don't let this happen to you. **Always review your contracts!** Make sure critical terms are present, and proactively identify and negotiate every landmine to prevent them from exploding when you least expect it. If you can prepare your own proactive forms, then by all means do so!

Contract Negotiation & Development Checklist

____ Develop standard, reusable templates for contracts that can be quickly deployed and are designed to protect your company's interests.

____ If your business counterpart insists on using their own form, review the contract thoroughly to make sure:

____ Business terms are correct (e.g., names, term, prices, quantity, specifications, delivery)

____ It is complete and fair for both parties

continued...

___ When conducting your contract review, pay special attention to the Dirty Baker's Dozen.

   ___ Use legal counsel to assist with negotiating any problematic sections to make them fair.

___ Once you have a fully-signed copy of the contract, store it in a centralized repository for easy access. Include all exhibits, attachments, and other documents that are part of the contract.

   ___ Monitor and perform all of your contractual obligations.

___ Develop pre-qualification standards before entering into a contract with your vendor or supplier to make sure they are able to:

   ___ Meet their contractual obligations

   ___ Deliver quality products or services

   ___ Adhere to regulatory requirements

   ___ Align with the ethical and operational standards of your business

___ Be flexible with your pre-qualification standards, taking into consideration things like the particular industry involved, types of products or services being sourced, size of the contract, and strategic importance of those products or services to your business.

3

COMPLIANCE POLICIES & TRAINING

Ask any executive at a Fortune 500 company what the functions of their compliance departments are, and you'll get a wide array of responses, all of which can be largely summarized as follows: "They make sure we comply with relevant laws."

That is a true statement when you're looking at things from a 10,000-foot view. There are numerous relevant laws, regulations, industry standards, contractual requirements, and generally-accepted best practices that must be followed across an enterprise to avoid trouble and ensure success. And that is why, not surprisingly, compliance is a full-time business function for almost every sophisticated global business.

But what if you're an entrepreneur or the owner of a small business? You probably don't have a compliance department. You may not even have a single, dedicated individual on your team to deal with compliance issues, even though you're still obligated to follow all relevant laws, regulations, and so forth. It's a lot to wrap your head around, and as you can imagine, legal and business requirements vary quite a bit from business to business and industry to industry. So where do you even begin?

Let's start with something every business cares about: *value*.

THE VALUE CHAIN

The concept of the "Value Chain" was developed by Michael Porter decades ago in his bestselling book *Competitive Advantage: Creating and Sustaining Superior Performance*. Porter's Value Chain model creates a high-level snapshot of all the activities in a particular business that combine to deliver value to the ultimate customers in some way, shape, or form. These functions include both the company's Support Activities and Primary Activities, all of which contribute to the profit margin the business hopes to gain.

At the highest level, Porter's Value Chain diagram looks something like this:

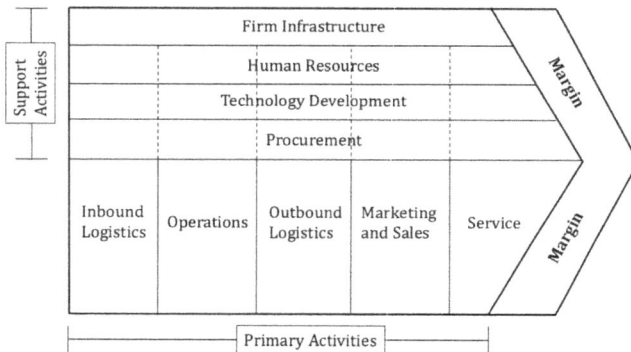

Using this framework, businesses can proactively identify the laws and regulations that affect each component of their respective enterprises. Once these issues are identified, they can then develop and implement standard operating policies and procedures to ensure compliance with their obligations, followed by robust and ongoing training.

Let's examine this process a little closer, starting from the top.

1) Support Activities

Let's suppose you're a startup athletic footwear manufacturer, and you're trying to get your arms around the vast compliance landscape affecting your growing business. Using Porter's Value Chain diagram, you can see that many different activities serve enterprise-wide business functions by improving efficiency and minimizing risks. Within these general Support Activities, the **Firm Infrastructure** component includes functions like finance, accounting, legal, and investor relations.

Within each of these functions, you have laws, regulations, and best practices that govern things like appropriate accounting standards, the financial information that must be disclosed by your business, how long certain business records must be kept, and the obligations of the business owners themselves, including fiduciary duties to each other.

Within **Human Resources,** you have numerous federal and state laws and regulations governing behavior in the workplace, with specific prohibitions against discrimination and harassment, as well as inappropriate hiring, disciplinary, and termination practices. There will likely be additional obligations about the number of hours employees are allowed to work, the number of breaks they must be given, overtime, and general working conditions.

Next, **Technology Development** centers largely around information technology (IT) and research and development. From an IT standpoint, this is where cybersecurity concerns arise. And since there are numerous international, federal, and state laws and regulations governing the storage and processing of confidential and personal data, security-related safeguards must be implemented—as well as notification requirements when a cyber event occurs. Your product research and development practices may also be subject to federal and state regulatory scrutiny to ensure that uniform standards are followed to protect the ultimate consumers of your products.

Finally, your purchasing practices (**Procurement**) are subject to certain laws, regulations, and best practices to ensure safe and sustainable materials and labor are being used in the manufacture of your footwear, particularly if that manufacturing takes place in a historically disadvantaged area (from a socio-economic standpoint).

Keep in mind, while governmental bodies may not explicitly require certain sourcing and material standards, that is no excuse for exploiting such loopholes. Your consumers will almost certainly find out, and when they do, your goodwill and credibility could be lost forever. In other words, compliance not only minimizes exposure to *legal* risks, but *business* risks as well.

Having explored the foundational Support Activities that underpin the operations of a business, we now shift our focus to the Primary Activities. These are the direct, value-adding activities that transform raw inputs into finished products and services, ultimately delivering them to the customer. While Support Activities ensure the business runs efficiently, Primary Activities are where the core business processes occur, directly impacting the product's journey from inception to the end consumer.

2) Primary Activities

As if there weren't enough laws, regulations, and standards for all your Support Activities within the Value Chain, many more are hiding in your Primary Activities. First consider your **Inbound Logistics** functions, which involve receiving raw materials at your factories for manufacturing footwear products. Whether you're procuring these materials overseas for domestic manufacturing or manufacturing the footwear overseas, you're likely subject to trade, customs, and border laws and regulations that require you to have certain shipment-related documentation in place in order to prevent product seizures. And depending on where you're manufacturing, you may also be subject to material sourcing and other requirements under existing trade agreements in order to receive preferential tariff treatment.

Your **Operations** functions can likewise be a source of significant copliance concerns, especially when your products involve manufacturing processes and machinery that could potentially injure employees. Federal and state occupational safety and health laws require the implementation of robust standards to prevent such injuries, including the availability of personal protective equipment (PPE) and regular safety training.

If your operations result in the discharge of waste products, you'll be further subject to federal and state environmental laws and regulations requiring appropriate testing, record-keeping, and reporting practices in addition to minimizing the discharge of any contaminants.

Your **Outbound Logistics** practices may also face legal scrutiny once your products have been manufactured and are ready for shipment— especially if you ship your products over highways. Whether you own or lease the vehicles transporting your products, you may be subject to transportation and driver safety laws and regulations. And even if you aren't subject to any such laws and regulations, your insurers will most likely require you to follow them anyway due to the rise of lawsuits and steep punitive damage awards.

Your **Marketing and Sales** practices will also be subject to numerous laws and regulations, such as banning you from making any false or misleading statements about your footwear products that might confuse or deceive customers. Other federal and state laws prohibit you from engaging in tactics that unfairly affect your competitors, as well as collaborating with competitors (or even your suppliers or customers) for anti-competitive purposes.

If you sell your products in other countries, there are additional laws and regulations prohibiting you from "wining and dining" foreign government officials to gain access to business there. Even if you don't realize at the time that they are government officials, it may not matter if you're caught.

Service functions, particularly with regard to how you assess recurring problems with your products post-sale, may also be subject to regulations and standards, as would the corrective and preventive actions you take in the field to minimize the likelihood of such defects in the future. Where laws and regulations don't apply, your contracts with customers may require you to pursue certain remedial actions due to express or implied warranties. Failing to do so could result in lawsuits and a loss of goodwill.

The above list is by no means exhaustive. Whether you sell athletic footwear or some other product—no matter what industry you're in—you need to make sure you fully understand the legal and regulatory landscape affecting your business, as well and the possible repercussions you could face if requirements are not met.

Here are just a handful of examples:

- To prevent Equal Employment Opportunity Commission (EEOC) investigations, claims, and lawsuits, you must comply with all applicable employment laws.

- To prevent sanctions, including the removal of your product from the market, you must comply with all relevant product-based regulations.

- To prevent sanctions and other losses caused by a data breach, you must comply with cybersecurity laws.

- To prevent suppliers from withholding key supplies or pursuing lawsuits, you must comply with all contract provisions.

- To prevent an unfriendly visit from the DOJ, you must comply with antitrust and anti-corruption laws.

- To prevent having your product intercepted and seized by Customs, you must comply with customs laws.

- To prevent a massive jury verdict that could end your business, you must comply with transportation laws and best practices.

- To prevent tariffs from being slapped on your products, you must comply with all requirements under the applicable free trade agreements in place.

And that is why most businesses hire compliance professionals to identify the vast galaxy of laws and regulations that could affect them. Those professionals can then help a business develop and implement policies and procedures to minimize their exposure to these potentially catastrophic legal and business risks.

These "ounces of prevention" can result in metric tons of cure. To illustrate this further, consider the following hypothetical scenario.

THE BALLAD OF CORY RUPSHIN

Conundrum, Inc., a growing medical device company, sells a product called Compli-X, which has radically innovated products currently in the market by being more broadly accessible and cost-effective.

Compli-X had been garnering attention and accolades across the US medical community and shows no signs of slowing down. In fact, the product has done so well that Conundrum owns most of the US market share for this type of device, and they believe there could be an international market for the product as well.

Conundrum's Vice President of Sales, Cory Rupshin, has some solid physician-customer contacts in India, China, and Brazil. An avid golfer, he rents out major golf resorts in each of these countries for "spare no expense" extravaganzas to lure these physicians in and convince them to start using Compli-X. It's the old "wine and dine on the company dime" approach, and Cory often brags to coworkers about the effectiveness of his expensive boondoggles.

Around the same time, Accelerate Corp. brings a product to market that is viewed as a direct and substantial competitor to Compli-X, particularly since it costs about 25% less. When Accelerate successfully rolls out its product in California, they finally appear on Cory's radar.

Seeing an imminent threat, Cory orders his company to sell Compli-X products below cost in California. Even though they will lose money doing this, he hopes to slow Accelerate's early momentum and force them out of the market. He also wants to send a message to any future competitors not to mess around with Conundrum.

Once his plan is enacted, Cory sits back in his big, padded chair, puts his feet up on the desk, and smiles.

The celebration is short-lived. Over the next month, he receives emails from a handful of Conundrum's customers in Florida that say they've been experiencing failures with Compli-X, requiring surgical intervention. He then receives more messages from physicians in New Jersey saying the same thing. And then one from Colorado. And even more from California! All told, the same issue with Compli-X has resulted in over a hundred patients needing surgical interventions.

Cory rushes downstairs to the office of Angie Neer, Conundrum's R&D specialist, demanding answers. After some additional testing, Angie discovers a few structural instabilities in Compli-X. Horrified, Cory realizes that their troubles have just begun!

After returning to his office, Cory looks at the financials to see how much money Compli-X brings in for Conundrum. It's a lot! In fact, the company largely depends on this one product for its own survival.

"We can't pull this product over a few failures," he mutters. "All the customer problems were probably the doctors' faults anyway. We can endure a few lawsuits, if it comes to that."

Cory is no rube. He completed one year of law school, and even though he dropped out, he thinks he knows a thing or two about handling legal problems. He manages to convince the CEO of Conundrum, Hedi Inna-Sand, that he can moonlight as the company's general counsel.

"Why spend $250,000 a year hiring a lawyer when I'm already here?" he says. "I went to law school!"

Sure enough, the lawsuits come, along with several requests for Conundrum to produce a log of all emails and records related to the Compli-X problems. As it turns out, Conundrum doesn't keep electronic records in the cloud, and the back-up tapes are cleared and rotated every thirty days.

"Good luck getting those emails," Cory says, chuckling to himself.

Conundrum's Director of Sales, Constance Ethyks, who reports directly to Cory, has become increasingly uneasy about the VP's actions related to Compli-X. She finally summons the courage to walk into his office and voice her concerns.

Cory smiles, gold tooth flashing, and gently warns Constance, "Do you have any idea how much business I bring in for this company? I'll fire you in a heartbeat if you say anything negative about me to anyone else. I'm *not* going to be taken down by some snot-nosed little girl."

Dejected, Constance walks out of his office. Just minutes after she leaves, Cory receives a call from CEO Inna-Sand asking him to come to her office to discuss a letter she's just received from reception.

"What does it say?" Cory asks anxiously.

"Well, Cory, it appears to be a subpoena from the DOJ about your Compli-X sales in India, China, and Brazil."

Back to the Real World

Most problem scenarios in your business won't be as clear, blatant, or pervasive as Cory's actions. However, there are many possible legal and regulatory exposures facing your company, and all of them necessitate some level of formal compliance. In the case of Conundrum, at least some of the following compliance policies would have prevented these problems had they been put in place (before "stuff" started hitting the fan):

- **Anti-Corruption Policy,** to prevent accusations of bribery of foreign and government officials, including Cory's extravagant golf outings.

- **Antitrust Policy,** to prevent Cory's illegal use of predatory pricing strategies to eliminate competition from Accelerate.

- **Adverse Event/Incident Reporting Policy** and **Corrective & Preventive Action Policy,** to ensure that all issues with Compli-X were appropriately reported to the FDA and that those issues were further corrected in the market, including a voluntary recall if necessary.

- **Record Retention Policy,** to ensure documents requested for litigation proceedings are not inadvertently (or unlawfully) destroyed in the normal course of business.

- **Anti-Harassment, Anti-Discrimination, and Anti-Bullying Policy,** with **Whistleblower** language, to prevent Cory's threatening behavior toward Constance and to further encourage Constance to come forward with information related to Cory's illegal practices.

And if they *really* wanted to be safe, Conundrum could have further minimized compliance exposure by creating the following:

- **Advertising and Marketing Approval Policy,** to ensure Compli-X promotional and instructional materials and product labeling contained appropriate language, including necessary product warnings and precautions.

- **Workplace Safety Policy,** to provide a safe and productive work environment for all employees on the manufacturing floor throughout the making of Compli-X.

- **Insurance Claim Reporting Policy,** to ensure timely and appropriate notification and shepherding of potential insurance claims involving Compli-X failures directly with the insurer.

- **Cybersecurity Policy,** to minimize Conundrum's legal and business exposure to cyber events (e.g., denial of service, data breach), particularly since they stored numerous confidential documents that could be accessed.

There are several other policies Conundrum could have considered putting in place by examining their own Value Chain, but you get the point.

Your company may not be a medical device manufacturer, and you may not sell any products like Compli-X (which doesn't really exist anyway). However, there are going to be numerous laws and regulations governing your specific industry and your Value Chain, and all of them need to be closely examined and considered. As the next case study will show, any one of these can blindside you if you're not paying attention.

Case Study: Icy Roads

That Friday morning started like any other: get up, work out, head to the office, drink a couple (four) cups of coffee, prepare a triaged list of pressing items for the day, and then get to work. About forty-five minutes into the first task, my list was disrupted when I received a call from a frantic new client:

> Client: "Hey, Chris, we just had an ICE[2] agent show up at one of our facilities."

> Me: "What happened?!"

> Client: "He said some of our product had been intercepted at the border, and he'd been asked to investigate further."

> Me: "Did he tell you why the product was intercepted?"

> Client: "He provided some paperwork detailing the issues and said he'd come back next week."

---

2   US Immigration and Customs Enforcement

Me: "Okay, please forward the paperwork and contact info to me, and I'll give him a call."

Client: "Thanks."

I received the paperwork shortly afterward and discovered that the issues centered around claims that my client's China-based manufacturer had mislabeled their products in violation of applicable US regulations. I contacted the manufacturer and advised them of the issue, further instructing them to stop all shipments while we conducted our own investigation.

The manufacturer was incredulous that there would be any problems and promised to send me copies of their design drawings and product photos, as well as a third-party certificate of compliance they had received.

While waiting for the documentation to arrive, I enlisted a former federal prosecutor with significant customs experience to join our team and provide guidance as to the seriousness of the investigation. We then contacted the ICE agent together to get more background on the earlier interception my client's products by Customs and Border Protection (CBP) and requested an extension to conduct our own internal investigation.

We established a good rapport with the agent, and he graciously gave us the following week for our investigation. He also provided contact information for the CBP counsel who was directing the inquiry, since he had little information himself except the initial paperwork that was provided to him.

Later that afternoon, we received the design drawings, photos, and certificate of compliance from the manufacturer. After reviewing the drawings and photos, I pulled the relevant regulations and discovered there was, in fact, labeling non-compliance. And as for the manufacturer's "certificate of compliance"? Well, where to begin? Unfortunately, it was:

1. Replete with typos and grammar issues

2. Issued by an Illinois-based company that we discovered had been involuntarily dissolved five years earlier and used an address that was listed online as a residential condominium for sale

In other words, the certificate was not credible.

I immediately notified my client and the manufacturer. The manufacturer pushed back, claiming there were no prior compliance issues with their other US-based customers. Nevertheless, they promised to immediately prepare and forward compliant design drawings for the company's approval, which we later reviewed and ultimately approved.

I then contacted the ICE agent to explain everything, advising him that there should be no further issues but asking him to let us know otherwise (as if they wouldn't!). We received confirmation from the Department of Homeland Security through the ICE agent that they would no longer be investigating the labeling issue. We then followed up with CBP, who confirmed that all remaining issues had been resolved for the time being.

Since then, products with the new labeling in place have been passing customs with flying colors, and life is good.

The Moral of the Story

Simply put, if the manufacturer had understood the regulations governing the labeling of their product and then reviewed the design drawings to ensure compliance with these regulations—rather than trusting dubious certifications—all of this could have been avoided.

Each year, non-compliance issues cost manufacturers billions of dollars in lost business, damaged reputation, and civil and criminal sanctions, among other things. To avoid these outcomes, big companies usually hire a Chief Compliance Officer (CCO) whose job it is to oversee compliance activities and alert senior management of systemic non-compliance issues, major regulatory changes, and the impact they might have on developing and marketing products. These officers serve as proactive "Doppler radars," ensuring that executives know what's going on so they can make educated decisions.

Even small- and mid-size companies are increasingly engaging and on-boarding compliance resources to provide guidance and oversight from the earliest research and development stages to the very end of the product lifecycle. This involves identifying relevant applicable laws and regulations, and then:

1.   Generating buy-in for compliance initiatives

2.   Developing written policies

3.   Regularly training company personnel on these policies in order to convey specific requirements, updates, and best practices

GETTING BUY-IN FOR COMPLIANCE POLICIES

As you may know from experience, business leaders—from entre-preneurs to senior executives—don't like being told they *can't* do something, or *must* do something, just because of a particular law or regulation. However, a new compliance policy will go over a lot easier if they understand the "why" of the policy in plain English—with no yawn-inducing legalese.

Therefore, when you implement a new compliance policy, it's a good idea to work with legal counsel to create a presentation that explains the new policy and its "why" to all key stakeholders in your organization. Personally, I like to create a **ninety-minute presentation** for stakeholders that begins with an educational background on the applicable law itself (as long as it's interesting enough to get their attention).

For example, when developing and implementing an antitrust compliance program, I may start with a history lesson on the rise of antitrust laws in the US that includes legendary figures like Teddy Roosevelt, John D. Rockefeller, Andrew Carnegie, and J.P. Morgan. Try to be entertaining and have fun with it. I always channel my old high school history teacher, Mr. Koester, who was adept at making even the most boring subjects sound interesting. Good storytelling will make the audience engage with the material.

After providing a bit of history, you can then discuss the laws themselves, including how they are enforced and what the penalties are for violation. If your audience already tuned out during your awesome history lesson, you may get their attention back by mentioning that criminal violations of the Sherman Antitrust Act are felonies punishable by up to ten years in prison and fines of up to $1 million per violation for individuals (up to $100 million per violation for corporations). That should make any business leader wake up and pay attention! To make it hit home a little harder, provide a few real-world horror stories of what can happen when you violate the law.

Let's say you're trying to get buy-in for a new anti-corruption policy. So you might tell the true story about how the DOJ knocked on the door of a medical device manufacturer named Smith & Nephew for using a Greek distributor to make improper payments to doctors at state-owned hospitals there. The DOJ considered this to be bribing government officials. The result? Smith & Nephew had to pay a $16.8 million fine and agree to a compliance monitor for eighteen months! Oh, yeah, and they also had to hand over $4 million in profits as well as nearly $1.4 million in prejudgment interest to resolve civil Securities Exchange Commission charges.

That should scare your audience a bit and *really* get their attention. Now, you can hit them with some easy-to-understand hypothetical situations, and then have them discuss whether the conduct in each scenario would constitute a violation. There's bound to be at least one devil's advocate who will argue the contrarian position. This is a good thing, because it proves that the presentation is being digested and thoughtfully considered. Try to incorporate as many people into the discussion as possible. Encourage cooperative dialogue and get everyone to think critically.

Throughout the presentation, reinforce that the information being provided isn't intended to make them experts on the particular law, only to help them spot potential issues in their own business dealings so they can be aware and proactively address them. Mention that you don't want them to be blindsided when they're asked to review and sign a written compliance policy later.

Compliance Policy Presentation Checklist

___ Start with a brief history of the law itself.

___ Discuss the law, including enforcement and penalties.

___ Share a few real-world horror stories about what can happen if you violate the law.

___ Have your audience discuss some easy-to-understand hypothetical scenarios.

DEVELOPING THE WRITTEN POLICY

Once you have buy-in for a new compliance policy among stakeholders, it's time to prepare the written policy. Again, you'll want to work with legal counsel on this. The document will serve as your front-line shield against any potential "knock on the door," but at the same time, it must be easy to read and comprehensible across the entire organization. Your lawyer may try to use indecipherable legalese, but make sure the document is written in *plain English!*

I recommend starting your policy with a letter from the owner (if you're a smaller company) or a high-ranking senior executive (if you're a larger company). In this letter, communicate the company's commitment to high ethical standards and your expectation that all policies be followed.

This establishes the significance and gravity of the policy. It's not just some random roadblock put up by the legal department.

Next, include a general, easy-to-read summary of the highlights of the policy. List the most important aspects ("*never* do this," "*always* do this," etc.), but don't go longer than a couple of pages.

After that, I recommend providing a statement that *briefly* explains the overarching, non-specific compliance guidelines, which should include some version of the following:

- Each employee is individually responsible for compliance with [the subject laws].

- Employees may not engage in, approve of, or tolerate any conduct violating [the subject laws].

- Employees in management positions are personally accountable not only for their own actions, but also for the conduct of their subordinates.

- Employees violating the policy may be subject to disciplinary action, including termination.

- Materials and education programs will be provided as needed to explain what's expected of employees related to their compliance obligations in connection with day-to-day responsibilities.

The next section should be a general overview of the laws themselves and all categories of enforcement and penalties for violation, followed by a more comprehensive list of the specific prohibitions and requirements. Again, this list should be in plain English and broken down into sections with an easy-to-read, bullet-point summary at the end of each.

Finally, the policy should conclude with a declaration that the policy isn't intended to make employees experts on the particular laws, but rather to assist them in understanding their compliance responsibilities, spot potential issues when they arise, and raise any red flags when necessary. Make sure to identify the person or department where questions or issues can be directed.

You'll also want to include a section at the end for each employee to sign, in which they explicitly acknowledge that they have received, read, and understand the policy; that they know where to go with any questions; and that they understand the consequences (i.e., disciplinary actions) of *not* following the policy.

Compliance Policy Checklist

___ Opening letter from the owner or a high-level executive

___ General, easy-to-read summary of the highlights of the policy

___ Statement that briefly explains the overarching, non-specific compliance guidelines

___ Have your audience discuss some easy-to-understand hypothetical scenarios

___ General overview of the laws themselves and categories of enforcement and penalties

___ Comprehensive list of the specific prohibitions and requirements

___ Declaration that the policy is not intended to make employees experts on the particular laws

___ Section for signature by the employee, acknowledging:

    ___ Receipt, review, and understanding of the policy

    ___ They know where to go with any questions

    ___ They understand the consequences of not following the policy

PROVIDING REGULAR AND MEANINGFUL TRAINING

Developing a robust written policy is only half the battle when it comes to creating a culture of compliance within your organization. You also have to provide regular and meaningful training to your employees to help them understand their obligations. Incorporate these meetings into their day-to-day responsibilities.

Most importantly, establishing a culture of compliance starts at the top, so owners, leaders, executives, and managers should lead by example. If you're a small company, you may be able to train each and every employee individually. If you're a larger company, this is probably either impractical or impossible; in which case, you can use learning management system (LMS) software that provides relevant modules to automate delivery, tracking, and administration of training to all relevant employees.

At a bare minimum, if you're a big enough company to warrant it, consider investing in some in-person training for management-level personnel. Then, make them personally accountable for training subordinates. All training should be well-documented to ensure enterprise-wide compliance, with regular auditing to ensure best practices. Consider using a third-party expert to audit compliance controls.

All of this contributes to a culture of compliance, where consideration of legal and regulatory exposures is incorporated into day-to-day business decision-making. And when an investigation or lawsuit inevitably commences, you can confidently demonstrate to the investigating body:

- Your company has written policies governing such infractions.

- You regularly educate your managers on those policies.

- You have a culture of compliance with the laws and regulations governing your industry.

This approach can and will minimize your exposure to worst-case outcomes.

Compliance Policies & Training Checklist

___ It's smart to have a department, team, or a dedicated individual to deal with compliance issues for your business. If you are a big company, this may be a Chief Compliance Officer (CCO).

___ Use Michael Porter's Value Chain to proactively identify the laws and regulations affecting each component of your company.

___ Once you have identified relevant applicable laws and regulations:

    ___ Generate buy-in for compliance initiatives by creating a presentation for stakeholders explaining each policy and its "why."

    ___ Work with legal counsel to develop written policies to ensure compliance obligations are met. Make sure the documents are written in plain English.

    ___ Provide regular training for employees to help them understand their compliance obligations, and then document that training. LMS software may help.

4

EMPLOYMENT PRACTICES

Your selection and treatment of employees are among the most crucial factors for your business's long-term growth and prosperity. Their productivity and happiness in the workplace will dictate the extent of your success.

Let that sink in.

So what can you do to keep your employees productive and happy? Well, first of all, don't be afraid to implement high onboarding and workplace standards, and to take decisive actions to hold everyone accountable to meeting those standards—including yourself! That means hiring the right people to solve your business needs, and then ensuring that those employees:

1. Are free from unfair and hostile treatment

2. Receive appropriate wages for their hard work

3. Work in a healthy and safe environment

4. Have plenty of opportunities for promotion and advancement

Let's look a little deeper at each of these.

IDENTIFYING AND HIRING FOR YOUR NEEDS

Regardless of the type of business you operate, you're going to have numerous problems that need solving—especially if your personal skillset mostly focuses on one specialty. Even if you fancy yourself a jack-of-all-trades, you need to focus on big-picture stuff. You can't delve into the minutiae; or you'll end up taking your eyes off the long-term prize.

The solution involves hiring skilled employees for executive, managerial, entry-level, and laborer positions. Provide them with the necessary resources to succeed, enabling them to contribute strategically and operationally towards your long-term vision.

The process of identifying and onboarding your ideal team begins well before the first interview. First, you need to clarify the problems most in need of solving. For example, let's suppose you're a startup apparel brand with two pressing issues facing your business:

1. You don't have enough time to regularly check with your supply chain to ensure consistent and predictable costs, delivery, and quality.

2. You're seeking to enter more diversified distribution networks to attract a broader range of prospective customers for your product lines.

How do you solve these two problems? Well, you certainly can't take care of it all by yourself, so you need to hire some skilled operations and sales employees to take care of them for you.

Now that you have a general idea of the kinds of people you need to hire, it's time to get more granular and determine exactly what you want each new employee to do. Get online and research what other similar companies are looking for when it comes to hiring and onboarding high-level operations and sales positions. In other words, read job openings on websites like LinkedIn, Indeed, or ZipRecruiter.

Just remember, there is no one-size-fits-all job description. You may not need every single thing that other companies require, so feel free to scale back (or add) to the job requirements. Make sure to include certain specifics of the employment, such as:

- If the position will be salaried or hourly, and what range you're willing to pay depending on the education, skills, and experience of the candidate.

- If there is a minimum level of education, skill, or experience that will be required for each position, and above that, if there is a preferred level.

- What benefits, such as relocation, insurance, vacation, and 401(k), you're going to offer.

- How much travel will be required for each position. Both operations and sales positions may require some travel, depending on supply chain locations, as well as the markets you're trying to reach.

- If you need your employees to be physically present at headquarters, or if you'll allow remote work or a work-from-home arrangement.

Once you have determined all of these things, you can use them to create a job description for each position. Turn those descriptions into job postings to let the world know that you're now hiring!

You'll need to include Equal Employment Opportunity (EEO) language in your posting to let prospective applicants know that your business gives people equal consideration regardless of their race, gender, background, culture, or identity. You can find numerous sample EEO statements on the internet, which you can use as a starting point to develop your own boilerplate language for all of your postings.

Here an example EEO statement:

We are committed to providing equal employment opportunities to all team members and applicants without regard to race, religion, color, sex, national origin, sexual orientation, citizenship status, uniform service member status, pregnancy (including childbirth, breast feeding, and related medical conditions), age, genetic information, disability, or any other protected status in accordance with all applicable federal, state, and local laws.

This policy extends to all aspects of our employment practices, including but not limited to recruiting, hiring, discipline, termination, promotions, transfers, compensation, benefits, training, leaves of absence, and other terms and conditions of employment.

You also need to develop an application form for people seeking to fill one of your job openings, but make sure the questions in your application are consistent with your EEO statement. You should avoid even the perception of discrimination, so beware of asking questions involving an applicant's personal traits or status which the law may protect (known as "protected characteristics" or "protected status").

The purpose of your application questions is to ask for information that will clarify their suitability for the position, so don't waste your or the applicant's time. Don't make applicants prepare long-form dissertations or answer a bunch of "What's the meaning of life?" type of questions, because neither of those are necessary for the operations and sales positions they want to fill. Worse, you might drive away some perfectly-qualified applicants.

Once you put your job listing out there into the world, you'll hopefully receive a bunch of responses from highly-qualified applicants. However, before you begin your first round of interviews, carefully review the resumes you've received with a critical eye. Resumes often present a "Hollywoodized" version of an applicant's educational and employment background. Try to read a bit between the lines.

If you request that prospective applicants provide references, make sure to follow up with them. Using the wonderful job description you've already created, compile a list of questions for each reference that will ensure the person you're interviewing has the talent and temperament to perform each required or desired duty (beyond the applicant's own biased perspective).

During the actual interview, I recommend asking the applicant what each reference would say about them, then compare what the applicant *thinks* they would say versus what the references *actually* said. Most applicants, except perhaps for a few masochists, are only going to list favorable references, so you might also ask the applicant what *negative* things each reference might say about them. This puts any potential problem areas out in the open early, and you get to assess the applicant's transparency and candor.

Remember, above all, your goal is to find out if a particular candidate can solve the operations or sales problems your business is facing, so you need to evaluate their education, skills, and experience, along with their professional temperament and overall fit for the position. That's what all of your questions need to revolve around. Never discuss a candidate's gender, race, or sexual orientation during the interview. These things should have no bearing on whether or not they can meet your business needs. Plus, it's against federal and state law to hire based on such protected characteristics, so you'll be opening up your business to investigation, claims, and litigation (which we will discuss in more detail later).

It's okay (even healthy) to discuss salary, wages, and benefits, but make sure you've done your research, so you know you're offering things that are consistent with market standards based on a candidate's education, skills, and experience. Failing to do so could expose you to claims of discriminatory hiring practices, particularly if you hire a less-qualified applicant without any protected characteristics over a more-qualified one with them.

Consider implementing an automated online pay equity service (e.g., Syndio, MarketPay, PayAnalytics, Parity Software) that can analyze particular jobs, compare them to similar positions across the country, and generate appropriate descriptions and potential discrepancies with your pay criteria—all in alignment with legal standards.

THE ONBOARDING PROCESS

When we talked about compliance in Chapter 3, we discussed the importance of regular training to help employees understand their obligations and incorporate them into their day-to-day work. This training should start on day one of a new hire's employment, and you need to weave it into their overall onboarding process.

Let's examine what this looks like.

Onboarding generally refers to an initial probationary period for a new hire, often their first ninety days on the job. During that time, your new employee will be:

- Drinking from a proverbial firehose of intensive orientation as they learn more about your business, including your history, facilities, competitors, suppliers, customers, key contracts, strategic issues, opportunities, and more.

- Meeting and more closely interacting with your staff on initial projects (bonus points if you introduce the new hire to your existing employees during the interview process to help determine their initial fit).

- Undergoing relevant, legally-required training, including learning about appropriate workplace behavior—such as avoiding and reporting harassment and discrimination (as we mentioned earlier, LMS software modules can efficiently curate and deliver appropriate training content, then track and administer completion).

- Reviewing and signing all necessary documents, such as employment terms and conditions, the employee handbook, and certain SOPs relevant to the business and job requirements.

You're going to end up investing substantial resources into developing this individual, so use the onboarding process to determine if your new employee is a good long-term fit for the job. If you notice any major red flags about their fit or performance, don't be afraid to pull the trigger and terminate sooner rather than later. Spare yourself, your business, and the unfortunate ill-fitting employee from a long, drawn-out, miserable experience.

Remember, we're talking about employment practices as a pillar of Preventive Law, so your onboarding process should be viewed as an opportunity to protect your business from potential future conflicts with an employee. Start developing and documenting your new employee's performance and adding those records to their file right away. After all, the honeymoon period sometimes ends just as quickly as it began.

KEEPING AN EMPLOYEE FILE

An employee file is a detailed record of an employee's relationship with your business. The primary purpose of keeping those records is to ensure that every employee's onboarding, training, performance, promotion, and perhaps even discipline are clearly documented.

By maintaining a complete file on each employee, you can separate legitimate employee claims against your company from frivolous claims filed by disgruntled workers. Look, let's be frank: there is no shortage of employment lawyers who are willing to represent disgruntled or aggrieved employees, as evidenced by the growing number of workplace harassment and employment discrimination claims and lawsuits across the country. Don't assume it won't happen to you—it happens to *many* businesses every year.

A complete employee file should include all tax-related documentation to be filed with governing bodies like the IRS, as well as *at least* the following documents:

1) Application & Hiring Documents

Every employee file should contain copies of that wonderful **job description** you developed as part of your initial posting. After all, your new hire applied as a result of that post, and they probably also included a **resume** and **references** to demonstrate why they were best suited for the job.

But what happens if you later discover that their submission contained falsehoods? Maybe the employee didn't really have the necessary education, skills, or experience they claimed to have. For that reason (among others), you want to keep documentary evidence that shows what the employee represented to you during the hiring process, so you can make sure it's consistent with their performance in the company.

Experts are split on whether or not you should include interview notes in an employee file. If you underline items for discussion on the resume, put an asterisk next to key items, or jot down names and contact numbers of references, then there shouldn't be any issue including such notes in the file. However, if you tend to write detailed accounts of each interview, including your own personal feelings about particular applicants, you may want to avoid including them. Your handwritten meandering could be interpreted by a lawyer as encroaching into protected characteristics territory during an employment discrimination lawsuit.

Include the **job offer letter** to the candidate, since it includes the pay and benefits you offered, as well as a printout of any **pay equity criteria analysis** that was performed. This will affirmatively demonstrate that your pay decision was not arbitrary, but rather developed by a well-respected third-party platform to ensure alignment with appropriate legal standards.

2) Onboarding Documents

As we discussed earlier, a new employee should go through an initial probationary onboarding period with all sorts of tasks they need to complete. First and foremost, depending on the nature of your business and the position, you may consider having them sign a copy of an **employment agreement**.

To use our earlier example, if your startup apparel brand incorporates groundbreaking new technologies that you have developed in-house, then you need to ask any new employee to keep that proprietary information confidential. You don't want them to leave and take this information to a competitor, or start their own athletic apparel brand by taking and using it.

A well-crafted employment agreement incorporates confidentiality language to protect your business, as well as other provisions to minimize exposure to your business in the event the employee resigns or is terminated. Just be aware that some jurisdictions may ban or limit non-compete language that restricts your ex-employee's ability to work for a competitor. In other words, to the extent you have such non-compete language in your standard employment agreement form, it may not ultimately be enforceable in a court of law if you happen to be in one of those unfortunate jurisdictions.

Your employment agreement should incorporate the terms of your company's standard **employee handbook** (which you should also have). The employee's file should include a copy of that handbook, along with a signed acknowledgement by the employee that they have read, understood, and accepted the terms and provisions.

While an employee handbook will be tailored to your needs, it should include some version of the following:

- Your company's overarching mission, vision, and values, as well as clear language that employment is "at will" (i.e., a general statement that your company may terminate the employee at any time for any or no reason, with or without advance notice).

- Your policy against unlawful harassment, discrimination, bullying, and retaliation, including examples of each, and what steps employees should take in the event they feel they have been victims of it.

- Your timekeeping and payroll practices, which should include working off the clock and overtime, as well as a clear requirement that hourly employees who use PPE as part of their job duties must clock in *before* putting on (or "donning") this PPE and then clock out *after* removing (or "doffing") this PPE. Failing to do so could expose your business to significant litigation, even a class action.

- A list of company benefits, including recognition of certain holidays, paid vacation, paid sick leave, workers' compensation, and training or educational assistance.

- A description of acceptable leaves of absence—particularly including Family and Medical Leave Act eligibility and conditions triggering leave—as well as how such leave is calculated, what happens if an employee fails to return after leave, and a recitation of what types of leave are *not* acceptable to your company.

- A description of general standards of conduct expected at your company (e.g., honesty, gifting to or from customers or suppliers, illegal activity, insubordination, use of company email and systems for personal reasons, smoking, attendance, workplace violence, political involvement in the workplace, appropriate dress and appearance in the workplace, romantic relationships in the workplace), as well as potential disciplinary measures for failing to adhere to such standards.

- Discussion of appropriate usage of personal mobile devices in the workplace, particularly if those devices are owned by your company, as well as a list of prohibited uses (including social media prohibitions), and any monitoring of systems which may be conducted to promote system integrity and minimize your company's exposure to data breaches or other cyber events.

- Discussion of the company's internal incident reporting and investigation policy, empowering employees to report any inappropriate or unlawful workplace behavior without fear of reprisal.

- An explanation of what will occur in the event of a separation of employment, whether voluntary or involuntary, including the extent to which any benefits will continue or terminate, the return of company property, eligibility for rehire, and exit interview procedures, if applicable.

As I've already said, the employee file should include an acknowledgement, signed and dated by each and every employee, that states the terms of the handbook were reviewed, understood, and accepted, and further that those terms may be changed with or without notice to the employee.

Now, what if you hire people *without* using an employee agreement or contract? While I don't recommend this, some businesses do operate this way. If you're not going to use an employee agreement, then consider developing a separate **confidential information policy** as well as the all-important **NDA** to protect your confidential and proprietary information and documents. As with other onboarding materials, make sure each employee reviews, understands, and accepts the terms by signing and dating an acknowledgement to be included in their employee file.

3) Job Performance

Beyond hiring and onboarding, it's important to document the employee's job performance over the course of their employment. This means conducting and documenting regular (typically annual) **performance evaluations**.

By now, you should understand the importance of being fair and consistent with your employees. Performance reviews are no different. Remember, your obligation to treat employees equitably under the law extends to the entire employment relationship, not just the hiring process. Use a standard set of performance criteria (e.g., attainment of goals, specific accomplishments, general productivity, quality of work, teamwork, leadership) for all employee reviews.

Third-party employee management software (e.g., BambooHR, Workday, Lattice) can help ensure consistency and fairness, minimizing the perception that your review process shows favoritism or is arbitrary. They also allow an employee's manager to conduct a self-review in advance of their performance review to identify any potential perception gaps that warrant further discussion.

By creating and maintaining a consistent review system, you also create opportunities for non-discriminatory promotion of employees within the company, especially when you also use a pay equity software platform. Keep a copy of any congratulatory **promotion letters** in the employee's file, as well as a printout of the employee's enhanced job description, responsibilities, and any relevant pay information analysis to ensure there are no pay discrepancies under the law.

Performance reviews identify the good, address opportunities for improvement, and document any discipline—up to and including termination of employment. Of course, employee discipline is uncomfortable and creates sticky issues for any business, which is why many companies use less draconian disciplinary measures like "performance improvement plans" in lieu of termination.

Rehabilitating a problematic employee can help you realize a return on investment in that employee, and you may find that there's a general lack of available qualified replacement talent. If you're going to use a progressive performance plan of training and coaching, followed by warnings, suspension, and eventually termination, then you run the risk of contradicting your "at will" statement in the employee handbook. It's okay to leave that language in the handbook as a safety net, but understand it could be used against you if you fail to terminate an employee as an immediate disciplinary measure.

Also, if you intend to implement progressive discipline, make sure the specific process is documented in the handbook, understood by new employees, and above all, consistently applied across all employees to minimize your exposure to claims of discrimination or wrongful termination.

Even with the most progressive disciplinary policy in the world, there are some behaviors and conduct in the workplace that *must* warrant immediate termination. Failing to do so could open your company up to liability (especially since you'll have had prior knowledge of such problematic behavior). Such instances will often be reported by another employee, so make sure to conduct ample investigation to validate or invalidate the allegations. Once again, consistent application will minimize your exposure to liability.

When an employee's journey with your company comes to an end, whether they're moving on or you've had to make the tough call, it's time to hand them their **separation letter**. When exactly should this letter make its appearance? Ideally, you'd present it right at the moment of separation or just before their last day, tailored to the situation's nuances. This document needs to nail down the separation date and clarify if the exit was their choice or yours.

For those cases where it wasn't voluntary, lay out the *why* behind their departure—be it downsizing, performance hiccups, or misconduct. Keep it factual and steer clear of any harsh critique. Remember, this could very well end up in court, and you want your company looking its best.

In this letter, you'll want to cover:

- Any final payments due, where to collect that last paycheck, and when

- The fate of their benefits—health, life insurance, retirement plans—and how they might continue, including the ins and outs of COBRA

- A checklist of company gear they need to return, like badges, keys, tech gadgets, etc.

And don't overlook informing IT to cut off their digital access to your networks.

At the same time, think about sliding them a **separation agreement**. This is where they agree not to sue over things like wrongful termination or discrimination, usually in exchange for some severance or other perks. But here's the thing, they might not sign. They could lawyer up, negotiate for more, or decide to take you to court. It's common, so keep your cool. Consider whether settling for a little extra is worth avoiding months, maybe years, of legal back-and-forth. Sometimes, standing your ground in court makes sense, but not always!

These documents are your legal safety nets when letting someone go. Team up with a savvy employment lawyer to craft templates that shield your company, ensuring all the legal bases are covered.

To summarize, an employee's file should serve as a comprehensive chronicle of their tenure with the company, documenting all significant employment-related events from onboarding to separation. In the event of legal proceedings, these documents will likely be required for review; maintaining organization and professionalism in these records is imperative. They must demonstrate your adherence to relevant legal standards and, if applicable, illustrate any consistent issues with the employee in question—which could prove crucial in defending the company against claims of misconduct.

Documents for the Employee File

____ Job Description, Resume, References

____ Job Offer Letter, Pay Equity Criteria Analysis

____ Employment Agreement, Employee Handbook

____ Confidential Information Policy, NDA (if no Employment Agreement)

____ Performance Evaluations

continued...

___ Promotion Letters (with Enhanced Job Description and Pay Equity Criteria Analysis)

___ Disciplinary Actions, Performance Improvement Plans

___ Separation Letter, Separation Agreement

___ Accident Reports, Return to Work Plans (next section)

___ Collective Bargaining Agreement (next section)

UNDERSTANDING WORKERS' COMPENSATION

Depending on the nature of your business, your employees might engage in tasks involving heavy machinery, chemical handling, or other hazardous activities, increasing the risk of workplace injuries or illnesses. When these incidents occur, employees are legally entitled to compensation. Most states mandate that employers carry workers' compensation insurance to cover these situations.

However, establishing whether an injury or illness is genuinely work-related isn't always straightforward. Consider a scenario where a new employee, tasked with stocking heavy product boxes, reports a sudden, severe back pain during a lift. Upon medical evaluation, it's revealed they have a history of similar issues, and HR discovers a previous, suspiciously similar workers' compensation claim at another job, where they were off work for over a year.

This scenario raises concerns about potential abuse of the system, often referred to as being a "professional claimant." Despite any suspicions you may have, the decision isn't yours to make. Instead, forward the injury claim to your workers' compensation insurer. It's their role to investigate, settle, or litigate the claim. This process underscores why you pay insurance premiums. Remember, it's the state, not you, that ultimately determines the compensability of a claim!

To mitigate such incidents proactively, consider the following measures:

- Examine if the injury could have been prevented through better training or safety measures, since a significant portion of workplace injuries (like back strains) can often be mitigated with proper techniques.

- Conduct regular safety training, which can significantly reduce workplace injuries and illnesses.

- Comply with Occupational Safety and Health Administration (OSHA) requirements, including:

  → Keeping detailed records of incidents (i.e., who was involved, job details, time, location, nature of the injury, and medical treatment received)

  → Providing PPE to reduce the likelihood and severity of injuries and illnesses

- Implement SOPs for tasks like lifting, PPE usage, and emergency responses to minimize risks.

Also consider developing and implementing "accident reporting" and "return to work" policies, which require your team to be proactive in the event of an injury or illness, including:

- Collecting all relevant details about the incident, including witness statements

- Obtaining a detailed medical report outlining what the employee can (and can't) do following an injury or illness

- Offering modified duties based on medical recommendations to facilitate their return (known as "transitional work")

- Collaborating with healthcare providers and the employee to tailor the return to work plan effectively

Make sure these policies are reviewed regularly by your employment lawyer to stay compliant with current laws and regulations. Following these policies will help your insurer evaluate and administer the claim. The return to work policy, in particular, not only aids in the employee's recovery but also maintains their skills and morale, while demonstrating your commitment to employee welfare and minimizing business disruption.

Implementing these steps can lead to fewer workers' compensation claims, potentially reducing your insurance costs and fostering a safer, more productive workplace. By proactively addressing safety and return-to-work strategies, you not only comply with legal requirements but also build a culture of care and resilience within your organization.

NAVIGATING UNION RELATIONS

Thus far, I've provided quite a bit of information on hiring, training, and employee treatment. Now, let's address a significant consideration: the dynamics change dramatically when dealing with unionized labor. When you're at the helm of a business with unionized employees, you're not just managing employees—you're navigating a complex agreement that dictates much of how you interact with your workforce.

First off, let's get one thing straight: **the Collective Bargaining Agreement (CBA) is your new bible**. It overrules any handbook or policy you've got lying around. If you're thinking about discipline or policy changes, the CBA's word is law, and you'll want to include a copy of that CBA in every union member's file—it's your roadmap through the union landscape.

Now, when it comes to introducing new policies, here's the deal: don't just drop them from above like a ton of bricks. The better approach would be to sit down with union leaders. You've got to talk it out, explain why these changes matter, and then negotiate. It's like a dance, and sometimes you'll step on each other's toes, but the goal is to move together. Once you've got an agreement, don't just throw the training at them. Make it a team effort, involving the union every step of the way.

Building a relationship with the union isn't just about avoiding grievances; it's about creating a partnership. Make a point to have regular meetings with union representatives. It's not all formal; sometimes, it's just coffee and a chat about how things are going. This keeps the air clear and the channels open.

When conflicts do pop up—and they will—you've got to handle them with care. Use what's in the CBA for resolution, or if it's silent on the matter, consider mediation or setting up a joint committee. It's about finding common ground, not winning an argument.

For those in management roles, training on union relations is crucial. A slip-up here isn't just an "oops" moment—it can land you in hot water with the National Labor Relations Board (NLRB), and nobody wants that kind of heat.

As the CBA approaches renewal, see it as an opportunity. It's your chance to refine terms, ensuring they grow with your business and the evolving workforce needs.

And here's a piece of advice: always keep the employee's perspective in mind. They're not just union members—they're the backbone of your operation. Understanding their rights and expectations isn't just good practice; it's good business.

In the end, managing union relations is about striving for that sweet spot where productivity meets harmony. It's not just about preventing problems—it's about creating an environment where everyone, union or not, can thrive. By implementing these strategies, you have a better chance of that happening.

Employment Practices Checklist

___ The first step to hiring skilled employees is to clarify the problems in your business most in need of solving.

continued...

____ Determine employment specifics:

    1) Salaried vs. hourly

    2) Minimum education, skills, or experience

    3) What benefits you will offer

    4) How much travel will be required

    5) Remote or on-site work, etc.

    ____ Use those specifics to craft a job description. Be sure to include EEO language.

    ____ Consider using an automated online pay equity service to set your salary and wages.

____ Develop an application form for people seeking to fill one of your job openings.

____ Conduct interviews of qualified candidates, but avoid asking questions that could expose your business to litigation (gender, race, sexual orientation, etc.).

____ The key goal of the onboarding process is to determine if your new employee is a good long-term fit for the job, so look for red flags.

____ Keep an employee file that provides a detailed record of every employee's relationship with your business, including documents related to application, hiring, onboarding, training, performance, promotion, discipline, and ultimately separation.

____ You're responsible for providing a safe and healthy work environment.

continued...

____ Develop and implement SOPs and training to minimize the likelihood and severity of injuries and illnesses in the workplace.

____ In the event of an injury or illness, your goal is to get the employee healthy and back to work (if possible), so develop and implement a "return to work" policy.

____ You're required to keep appropriate records in the event of an injury, illness, or fatality.

____ If you work with union employees, remember to always follow the default requirements of the CBA first and foremost.

____ Any new policies, procedures, and training must be discussed and negotiated with the union.

____ Build a relationship with the union by having regular meetings, training managers on union relations, and keeping the employee's perspective in mind.

5

INSURANCE

L et's be honest: talking about insurance is about as exciting as watching
paint dry. But as a business leader, it's a topic you need to understand.
There's no getting around it. I'll try to make it as interesting as I can,
but I suggest a couple shots of espresso right now before we get into it.

Okay, ready? Here we go.

Imagine your company suffers a big loss when several of your products
are discovered to be defective, resulting in a series of injuries to your
customers and ultimately a product recall. It's a big blow, but you're not
stressed out. After all, you're insured. This is exactly why you've been
paying all of those premiums, right? But then you file your claim, and
your claim is denied. The insurance company isn't going to cover any
of it.

You feel frustrated and helpless. How could the claim have been
denied? You just don't understand. Where did you go wrong? You
wonder if you maybe failed to select the type of insurance you needed,
or maybe the loss was listed as an exclusion in the fine print of your
insurance policy. Maybe it was denied because you didn't file your
claim soon enough. Or perhaps the insurer has a strange interpretation of a specific provision tucked deep inside the maze of paragraphs.

All of these are possible, and they can all be avoided.

Or what if your claim is accepted, but it involves defending litigation against those injured customers in court? In most cases, your insurer will assign one of their lawyers to defend you. However, without proper oversight, the insurer and their counsel may decide to use a litigation strategy that isn't in your best interests. As you'll see in Chapter 6, scenarios like this can and do happen.

I've seen too many cases throughout my career where an insured business owner's interests were the last things being protected. And unfortunately, litigation can lead to skyrocketing premiums at renewal, or worse: a loss of insurance coverage altogether. I've seen that far too many times as well.

SO HOW DOES INSURANCE WORK?

After reading the previous paragraphs, you may be furious, thinking, "How can insurers be so unfair? We pay them a lot of money just for them to stab us in the back!"

To be fair to insurers, theirs is a for-profit industry, so it might be helpful to explain how insurance works. Insurance isn't exactly what some people think it is, but maybe if you understand it a little better, it'll help you get the most value out of it.

Recall our discussion about Porter's Value Chain, which helps identify potential compliance issues across your Support Activities and Primary Activities. The same model can also be used to identify potential business risks you face. If you're a product manufacturer, for example, your business risks might include:

- Design, manufacturing, or pricing barriers

- Delay or failure of product to get to its ultimate destination in a timely manner, whether due to supply chain failures or regulatory issues

- Improper marketing, resulting in diminished customer goodwill

- Problems at headquarters or within individual departments, such as rampant employment issues or a data breach

- Natural disasters destroying key facilities

How can you deal with these areas of risk once you've identified them? First, you can determine the respective likelihood, severity, and velocity of each one and compare them to the cost (and burden) of implementing preventive measures.

Remember Cory Rupshin, our corrupt pharma executive who was bribing foreign doctors with expensive golf outings? Cory may have rated the likelihood of his bribes harming the business as relatively low, since he didn't expect to get caught. However, the severity of harm due to his actions was off the charts; and indeed, his actions would eventually result in crippling fines and penalties for the business. Moreover, the velocity of harm was also quite high, since the DOJ moved swiftly in their investigation and subsequent punitive measures.

Therefore, stopping Cory's corrupt behavior by implementing an Anti-Corruption Policy should have been of utmost importance to prevent future occurrences.

You may not have a Cory Rupshin working in your business (at least I hope not!), but you still need to cast a wide net to identify and analyze the risks across your business. Assemble a cross-functional team to help you with this process, analyzing your own Value Chain to look at your Primary and Support Activities. Then you need to determine your risk appetite, risk tolerance, and risk capacity.

- **Risk Appetite**: the level of risk you're willing to accept without much mitigation or monitoring.

- **Risk Tolerance**: the point at which you're going to develop steps to reduce or mitigate the risks.

- **Risk Capacity**: the threshold where you'll absolutely not accept the risks under any circumstance, and will therefore take all possible steps to prevent or avoid them altogether.

So where does insurance enter the picture? Well, some risks that rise beyond your risk capacity may be transferred to a third party who is willing to take them from you. Insurance serves as a primary mechanism for taking on these unwanted risks. The insurance industry has developed over the course of centuries to become an effective marketplace for the "buying" and "selling" of risks.

Insurance premiums are the fees you pay for an insurance company to accept a particular risk (or set of risks), and your insurance policy is a contract containing the terms in which the insurer is willing to accept the risk. Furthermore, there are different types of insurance for the different types of risks.

So what types of insurance does your business need to carry? Workers' compensation insurance is mandated in most states, and some level of commercial auto insurance will probably also be legally required. Depending on the nature of your business, you may need some combination of the following as well:

- Commercial property

- Business interruption

- Commercial auto liability

- Commercial general liability

- Products liability

- Employment practices liability

- Workers' compensation & employers' liability

- Cargo & stock throughput

- Cybersecurity

- Directors & officers' liability

- Errors & omissions

- Fiduciary liability

- Crime

- Kidnap, ransom & extortion

- Environmental & pollution

- Marine vessel hull & liability

Remember, when you purchase an insurance policy, the insurer is making a calculated gamble that you won't have any loss related to that risk. That is the only reason why insurance companies are able to make money at this. Therefore, if you do experience a major loss, or numerous small losses during the policy term, insurance payouts may exceed the amount of premium you've paid. At that point, you become a money-loser to the insurance company.

That's why insurers are careful about the risks they accept, and they use robust underwriting departments to do "full cavity searches" of your business before they decide whether or not to accept a particular set of risks. And before they accept the risk transfer, they subject you to a voluminous policy contract that contains numerous coverage exclusions, as well as ambiguous legalese provisions written by teams of lawyers. Sometimes, this confusing language can make an insurer's obligation to compensate you for a specific loss open to interpretation (more on that later).

As an applicant, you're generally classified as *standard*, *substandard*, or *declined* risk based on your level of business risk. If your business is considered a higher (substandard) risk class by the underwriting department, you're going to be charged a higher premium, while a business in a lower (standard) risk class will be charged a lower premium for the same kind of coverage. Why? Because the insurance company believes you're more likely to experience a compensable loss. And if your risk is seen as too high, you may be declined insurance altogether.

If too many businesses suffer misfortunes relative to the total number of insured businesses (e.g., in the case of a hurricane or wildfire), then overall premiums will be raised for all policyholders. This ensures that policyholders can collect, but it also keeps insurers in business.

As we said, insurance is a for-profit industry, and insurance premiums are the primary way they make revenue. Insurance companies must be mindful of their overall "loss ratio": the balance of premium revenue vs. loss payout. If payouts across their portfolio outweigh revenue, then that insurance company might become insolvent.

Obviously, insurance companies want to stay in business just as much as you do, so you can understand why they are cautious about paying out for a major loss.

DON'T WAIT TO GET INSURED

To be clear, even though insurance is a for-profit industry, you still need it! No one can safely operate a business without plenty of relevant insurance coverage. Otherwise, a single lawsuit or major loss could wipe out your business.

Unfortunately, many business leaders put off procuring or renewing their business insurance until the last second because they have so many other things to focus on. When they finally end up getting insurance, they often purchase policies and start paying premiums without really knowing what their policies cover (and don't cover).

At the start of your business and every year after that, you need to proactively determine the types and amounts of insurance that your business needs. Work with an experienced broker who understands your risk profile and ensures you have appropriate, sufficient, and cost-effective coverage.

I recommend using the following process. First, set up an initial strategy meeting with your broker around **120 days** prior to purchasing or renewing insurance. During this initial meeting, discuss any insurable loss events that have occurred during the year (making sure the insurer has been notified of them). Then explore current market conditions in the insurance industry, including premium increases you may be facing at renewal. Remember, insurers rarely lower premiums unless your risk exposure dramatically decreases for some reason.

Is it necessary to work with a specialized broker? Not necessarily, but a sophisticated commercial insurance brokerage firm should be able to effectively aggregate data from both the insurance industry and their own clients, helping you manage expectations and develop a better strategy.

About **90 days** before you have to purchase or renew your insurance policy, you should receive applications from the insurance company. Spend the next thirty days or so making sure the applications are complete and accurate. Your broker should pre-fill most of the information from the previous year, though your financial and operational information will need to be reviewed and updated as needed. Review and discuss your loss history with your broker at this time, so they can effectively "sell your story" to the insurance marketplace.

About **60 days** before you have to purchase or renew your policy—and assuming you've updated your applications by now—your broker will take your applications to market to gauge responses from insurance companies. If you already have established relationships with specific insurers, they may respond quickly.

However, remember, insurers are gambling that they won't lose money when they take on your risk. An insurer may still renew your insurance if you've had a large loss, as long as that loss was truly unforeseen. However, if you seem like a money loser, they may raise your premium significantly or simply decline to renew you.

Business relationships matter, and that includes your relationships with your insurers. The longer the relationship, the more data they will have to understand the risk you pose, which can lead to more competitive pricing. However, if one of your insurers just paid out major losses on your behalf, they may decide they've had enough of your risk and refuse to renew you. Just be prepared for the possibility.

By the time it's **30 days** until renewal, you should have some responses from the insurance marketplace. At that point, you need to sit down with your broker and evaluate the best options. Then let your chosen insurers know that you're going to be transferring your risks to them and paying the premium (a process called "binding coverage"). They will offer temporary contracts called "insurance binders" that will provide coverage for the specific risks placed with them while you wait for the official policies to be issued. Make sure to closely review your insurance binders to see that they align with your expectations, and discuss with your broker if they don't.

You should hopefully receive copies of your insurance policies in the next **30 – 45 days following** renewal. Have your broker go over the policies to ensure all necessary and expected coverage items are included, that all coverage add-ons (called "endorsements") are in place, and any vague or ambiguous provisions are clarified in advance (more on that later).

Now, to be clear, this process doesn't always go as smoothly as I've made it sound, though it should be an aspirational goal for your business over the long term. To help you make the process smoother, we're going to look a little deeper at some key aspects of procuring and renewing insurance, beginning with determining your risk capacity.

FIGURE OUT YOUR RISK PROFILE

There's an important interplay between your risk capacity and the risk transfer your insurance carrier is willing to accept. For example, the insurer may tell you that they will provide $10 million in coverage subject to a $250,000 deductible. That means the insurer's obligation doesn't trigger until your company has shelled out the first $250,000 in loss recovery for a specific insurable event. In doing this, the insurance company is dictating a specific point at which your risk transfer will take place.

You need to figure out what risk transfer points on each line of insurance coverage make sense for your business's risk capacity and organizational goals. Take a look at the different policies you're purchasing and review the limits and deductibles currently in place. Consider and discuss with your team the likelihood and severity of worst-case scenarios that could trigger coverage on each line, as well as the financial impact to your company on the off chance one occurs.

As an example, let's say you're a product manufacturer and had historically purchased property insurance to cover a key production facility up to $5 million, with a $25,000 deductible in place. You initially rationalized this decision by pointing to the value of building itself and the estimated cost to replace it. As far as the $25,000 deductible (risk transfer point) that you selected, it was largely arbitrary and not based on any analysis or methodology.

This time around, however, you astutely go to your operations and finance teams to better understand how a catastrophic fire or storm at this facility might affect the company's overall balance sheet. After all, a shutdown at this facility would inevitably result in some level of lost business income (which is also covered under your property policy).

Your operations team lets you know that a backup facility would be able to shoulder the added burden in a worst-case scenario, but it would take up to six months to transfer production there. Even worse, your finance team lets you know that business income losses during this shutdown period could reach $30 million. In other words, this shutdown could mean bankruptcy.

Sitting down with your finance team and insurance broker, you learn that increasing existing coverage to this level on an annual basis would be cost-prohibitive. However, increasing your deductible from $25,000 to $1 million—and then insuring the facility for the $5 million in property loss plus another $25 million in business income loss—was a much more manageable solution. Your finance team confirms the company would be able to sustain the first $1 million in losses following a worst-case scenario, as well as the $5 million hit over the $25 million policy limit in such an unlikely event.

By conducting this analysis early in the process, you effectively determined that the more appropriate risk transfer point on this facility was actually $1 million (not the arbitrary $25,000). And then by working with your teams to align coverage with worst-case exposure given this risk transfer point, you have saved your business from potential extinction!

THE BIG PICTURE IS NOT ENOUGH

Now, one of the biggest problems I see when it comes to business insurance is that far too many companies simply don't know what's contained within their insurance policies. They get a big picture idea of what should be in there, then they sign the policy and simply assume (and hope) that they will be covered if something bad happens.

In other instances, I've seen companies swallow the entire cost for some big loss, only to later discover that the loss could have been covered by one of their insurance policies.

To be fair, as with so many legal documents, the legalese contained in many insurance policies is simply indecipherable for anyone other than a sophisticated broker or lawyer. Still, you have to make sure a policy aligns with your business needs before you sign. Leveraging those professionals to help you analyze, select the right policy, and negotiate your insurance program could save you a lot more money and headache down the road!

As I've said, an ounce of prevention is worth a metric ton of cure.

Not long ago, I worked with a product manufacturer whose primary factory was based in the Philippines, with suppliers based in two other Asian countries. They shipped their products from their factories to a warehouse in the US via ocean cargo.

When I reviewed their insurance policy, I discovered that it only covered losses that occurred in the US, US territories, and Canada. That meant if their primary factory shut down, they couldn't recover any lost income resulting from delayed production. But even if the policy *had* covered the Philippines, there were exclusions for earthquakes, tsunamis, floods, and labor issues. That removed a huge number of risks that could occur in the Philippines.

Moreover, the policy only covered the company's "direct suppliers," which excluded disruptions at their material suppliers. To top it all off, there was no marine cargo policy in place, so shipments lost at sea were not covered.

The company had *no idea* that there were such huge gaps in their coverage until I reviewed the policy. Can you imagine how shocked company leaders would have been if they'd lost a shipment at sea only to discover after the fact that none of the loss was covered by their insurer? Yet these kinds of insurance surprises happen all the time in the business world.

I can't overstate the importance of having a *comprehensive* understanding of what your insurance policies cover (and don't cover). There are a lot of questions to consider. Does your policy cover natural disasters, geopolitical turmoil, or labor strikes? How complex are your supply chain, logistics, and distribution networks, and is business interruption coverage protecting all of them?

Does your cyber-insurance policy adequately cover the number of electronic data records you're storing, including all customer data and credit card information taken as part of direct-to-consumer sales? With the rise of politically-oriented cyberattacks, do you have cyber-terrorism coverage in place?

Do you have overlapping coverage in more than one policy that could trigger an "other insurance" clause in one or more of them? Are there exclusions in your insurance policy that create gaps in your coverage?

Is your policy **occurrence-based** or **claims-made**? In a "claims-made" policy, you're required to notify your insurer of potential liability (i.e., a claim) as a precondition to the insurer's obligation to cover that claim, and that notice is required to be given the same policy year that the claim occurs. On the other hand, an "occurrence" policy covers claims that "occur" during the policy year, regardless of whether or not you report that claim to your insurer during that same policy year.

As you can imagine, there is more exposure to the insurer by issuing occurrence policies, and therefore insurers will likely charge more premium for them. Occurrence policies are more common in commercial auto and property settings, while claims-made policy options are more common when the insurer is covering claims by a third-party against you (e.g., product liability claims).

Let's suppose you're a medical device manufacturer that makes back screws, and one of your screws breaks, resulting in a paralyzed patient. That patient files a multi-million-dollar lawsuit against you, so you hire a $600-an-hour attorney to defend you. Litigation lasts over three years, but on the eve of trial, you have the opportunity to settle the case for $5 million (or roll the dice at trial and potentially lose much more). Realizing you have product liability insurance which could cover that massive settlement, you decide to send a letter to the insurer for coverage.

For three years, the insurer has been unaware of this situation, and they've lost the opportunity to use their own network of attorneys to defend the case. This is unfortunate, because insurers are naturally able to negotiate lower attorney rates given their size and volume of cases. It's grossly unfair of you to surprise the insurer with this coverage request three years after you knew about the lawsuit—especially when a $5 million settlement is staring you in the face on the eve of trial.

This is why claims-made policies exist. They put a notice window on you as a prerequisite to coverage.

Now, to be completely candid, most occurrence policies wouldn't cover the above scenario anyway, since there are still requirements that you notify within a "reasonable time"—and three years isn't reasonable.

While timely notification is critical in claims-made policies, understanding the nuanced definitions within your insurance policy can be equally crucial, as illustrated by the following real-life case study where an honest mistake in interpreting policy language led to significant financial exposure.

Case Study #1: Communication Gap

A product company manufactured and sold a type of implantable medical device. Since these products could potentially cause injuries to end users (i.e., patients), the company smartly purchased a Products-Completed General Liability insurance policy to cover any claims made by patients. The policy had an overall limit of $10 million, with a deductible of $100,000 per occurrence. An "occurrence" was defined in the policy as "the continuous or repeated exposure to substantially the same general harmful conditions, all of which will be deemed to arise out of the same occurrence."

That's some "clear as mud" legalese, and it's exactly the kind of stuff you have to wade through when seeking clarity about your coverage. Not surprisingly, the product company didn't fully understand the ramifications of this definition of "occurrence."

A few months later, it was discovered that one particular surgeon, who had implanted the company's device in numerous patients at the same hospital over the course of several weeks, had misinterpreted certain guidance provided in the surgical technique manuals developed by the company. Unfortunately, this resulted in fifty-two patients suffering similar injuries from the product failing after surgery.

These patients then sued the surgeon, the hospital, and ultimately the product company. The company determined that each case could be worth at least $100,000, or $5.2 million in total. However, they breathed a sigh of relief and patted themselves on the back for having the foresight to purchase $10 million in insurance coverage—more than enough to cover all of these lawsuits. They notified their insurer and requested coverage under the policy.

The insurer sent the company a response letter that seemed to be good news, as they announced that they would indeed be covering the claim. However, a few paragraphs later, the good news became catastrophic. The insurer informed the company that they were interpreting the definition of "occurrence" in the policy to mean that there were fifty-two separate lawsuits triggering *fifty-two separate deductibles* before any coverage would attach.

After doing the math, the company realized that the insurer's interpretation meant their coverage wouldn't kick in until at least $5.2 million in aggregate losses had accumulated. In other words, the insurer had sneakily created a $5.2 million gap in coverage. In essence, there was effectively no coverage for these claims, and the company would be left to pay everything out of pocket.

They decided to send a letter back to the insurer arguing that the group of claims clearly "arise out of the same occurrence" under the definition. Specifically, the same surgery was performed by the same surgeon at the same hospital using the same product, repeated fifty-two times. As such, the company asserted, there was "continuous or repeated exposure to substantially the same general harmful conditions."

Ultimately, the insurer refused to back down from their position, and the company was forced to consider spending additional hundreds of thousands of dollars suing the insurer over their interpretation of this definition.

DEALING WITH THE LEGALESE IN POLICIES

Understanding the dense legal language in insurance policies can prevent scenarios like that of the medical device company, ensuring you're not caught off guard by coverage gaps. Now, let's apply this understanding to a critical area where clarity in policy language is paramount: cybersecurity.

Cybersecurity consistently ranks among the top risks for global businesses, as highlighted in the annual Allianz Risk Barometer. Here's what you need to know:

- **First-party cyber insurance** typically covers direct losses from a cyber incident, like the costs for data recovery, customer notifications, credit monitoring services, and business interruption losses.

- **Third-party cyber insurance** protects against costs associated with legal defense, settlements, judgments, and regulatory fines stemming from a cyber event.

However, like all insurance policies, your cyber policy is likely riddled with complex, ambiguous language, not to mention gaps and exclusions that could catch you off guard.

When you're aiming to clarify and negotiate the legalese in your cyber insurance policy, keep an eye out for these eight key items, along with strategies to ensure your policy truly supports your business in the wake of a cyber incident:

1) Adequate Limits & Sub-limits

According to the 2024 "Cost of a Data Breach Report" conducted by the Ponemon Institute (sponsored by IBM Security), the average cost of a data breach to US businesses is $9.36 million.[3] To determine the potential cost of your own exposure, you need to audit the number of research and development records you have, as well as employee information, business-to-business and individual customer data, and other confidential records and information that could potentially be damaged or stolen.

Then examine your cyber insurance policy to determine if the aggregate policy limit and sub-limits of coverage will adequately protect your

---

3   https://www.ibm.com/reports/data-breach

exposure. The aggregate limit refers to the absolute most the insurance company will pay in the event of a breach. Sub-limits set caps for certain types of losses or costs related to an insurable event, which are often much lower than the overall aggregate limit itself and can blindside you.

For example, you may have a cyber insurance policy with a $5 million aggregate limit, which is subject to a $1 million sub-limit for regulatory fines or penalties assessed by a governing body against you (which we'll discuss shortly). If you receive a $3 million fine as a result your failure to appropriately secure data or notify customers, you'll actually pay $2 million of that loss out of your own pocket, regardless of that $5 million aggregate limit you thought would protect you!

2) Business Interruption Coverage

One of the biggest components of loss during a cyber event is the loss of business that results from network systems shutting down. These business interruptions are often subject to sub-limits in your cyber policy. As part of your audit of the cyber policy, it's important to evaluate the potential total loss of business income you might experience from a network shutdown to determine if the policy coverage is adequate.

Just note, there may be additional sub-limits within this business interruption sub-limit, such as the waiting period (the amount of time you must wait before coverage begins) and the period of restoration (how long it takes before your systems are returned to normal). You can only recover business income loss within that window, so make sure each of these are adequate as well. Be ready to negotiate changes to make the policy more suitable for your needs.

To further reduce your exposure to business interruption losses, consider contingency plans like storing information and data on physical servers and cloud-based backups.

3) Coverage for Fines and Penalties

Companies are legally required to comply with data protection and breach notification standards, and subject to penalties and fines for failing to do so. These include the Sarbanes-Oxley Act, Gramm-Leach-Bliley Act, PCI Data Security Standards, HITECH Act, SEC Guidance, FTC Act, Fair Credit Reporting Act, Executive Order 13636, laws in all fifty states plus the District of Columbia, Puerto Rico, and Guam, as well as international laws (e.g., EU, Asia, South America, Middle East).

Indeed, Equifax was fined at least $575 million by the Federal Trade Commission (FTC), Consumer Financial Protection Bureau (CFPB), and all fifty states and territories for failing to secure their networks adequately during 2017, resulting in a data breach affecting nearly 150 million people.

Fines and penalties can result in massive exposure from a cyber event, and your cyber policy may limit or exclude coverage for them. Make sure adequate coverage is in place in your policy. Furthermore, make sure you have written policies and procedures in place (along with regular and meaningful training) to ensure reasonable compliance with data protection and notification laws. This should minimize not only your exposure to a cyber event, but also your overall premium costs as well.

4) Contract Exclusion

Many cyber insurance policies exclude coverage for claims based on you assuming liabilities for others pursuant to contracts.

Let's suppose a data breach occurs, and numerous third-party records maintained by your company are compromised. A series of lawsuits ensues, with some of these third parties claiming that you contractually assumed the responsibility for safeguarding their confidential information maintained on your systems. If this contract exclusion exists in your insurance policy, these claims wouldn't be covered.

To avoid this potentially catastrophic scenario, make sure you don't assume any impractical cybersecurity requirements in your third-party contracts. Look closely at the reasonableness of the indemnification and insurance language in those contracts. Once you get your third-party contracts squared away, try to negotiate "insured contract" coverage for instances where you've agreed to indemnify certain customers or clients for these kinds of losses.

5) State-Sponsored Acts Exclusion

Many cyber insurance policies exclude claims based on actions authorized or supported by foreign authorities. Given how broadly some of these exclusions are written, any otherwise-covered cyber event supported in any way by a foreign government could potentially be excluded from coverage.

According to a study by Carbon Black, a global cybersecurity vendor, 41% of their investigations reveal that cyber events originated in either China or Russia, with many of the remaining attacks coming from Iran, North Korea, Pakistan, and Vietnam.[4] An insurer could argue that a cyber event presumptively involves action by one of these government authorities, and therefore coverage is excluded under your cyber insurance policy.

Use the NotPetya and WannaCry ransomware attacks and the Marriott data breach (which were attributed to Russia, North Korea, and China, respectively) to test if your insurer would provide coverage in these scenarios. If not, then you may want to consider coverage endorsements (or alternative insurance carriers entirely) to proactively address these massive uncertainties.

---

4   https://news.vmware.com/releases/carbon-black-threat-report-reveals-destructive-cyberattacks-increasing-ahead-of-2018-us-midterm-elections

6) Prior Acts Coverage (Retroactive Date)

Let's suppose you had cyber insurance in place for policy year January 1, 2024 to January 1, 2025. You receive a call in October 2024 from law enforcement warning that your systems have been breached. Upon further investigation, you learn the breach resulted from an officer clicking on a link in December 2023 and giving a password to a hacker who claimed to be someone from your IT department.

Since the breach occurred in December 2023, before your policy's effective date, your losses might not be covered unless you have Prior Acts coverage with a retroactive date before December 2023. Hackers can reside in systems for months, if not years, so it's always best to have retroactive dates as far back as commercially feasible.

As part of your robust cyber insurance audit, explore appropriate retroactive dates, and make sure they are specifically identified in your insurance policy before a claim occurs.

7) Losses Absent an Actual Cyber Event

Most cyber insurance policies provide coverage *only* in the event of an actual infringement, privacy violation, security breach, or disclosure of personal information. However, some businesses have faced litigation even in the absence of an actual cyber event.

One example is the case of *Jason Shore and Coinabul, LLC v. Johnson & Bell, Ltd.* An Illinois law firm's clients learned that the firm had certain data security flaws, exploitable out-of-date software, and vulnerable VPN and email systems, so they initiated a class action lawsuit against the firm, accusing them of a failure to properly secure client data that "subjected the plaintiffs to an increased risk of injuries."

The thing is, there had been no actual cyber incident! No actual intrusion, data exposure, or data misuse! It didn't matter. The firm was still required to spend significant funds defending themselves in court.

It could happen to you too, so explore coverage options with your insurance carrier for such scenarios. Keep in mind, the contract exclusion issues mentioned above may also come into play depending on the liabilities you assume for your clients and members.

8) Overlapping Provisions

Some items that are covered in a stand-alone cyber insurance policy may also be covered in your other insurance policies. For example, business interruption coverage may also exist in your property policy, privacy-based claims may also be covered in your commercial general liability policy, employee negligence in causing a breach may also be covered in your professional liability (E&O) policy, and computer fraud may also be covered under your crime policy.

"Other insurance" clauses in insurance policies are provisions that address what happens when there is more than one policy covering the same loss—and attempt to prioritize how those claims might be handled. However, when these clauses conflict (i.e., both policies claim to be excess over the other), it can lead to litigation between the insurance companies, leaving you in limbo while you wait for that much-needed coverage.

These provisions may also include "pro-rata" language, in which each insurer will only pay a subjectively determined portion of your overall loss, preventing you from full recovery. Some policies may even include "escape clauses," effectively allowing an insurer to avoid paying a claim altogether if a competing policy is available to cover the loss.

To avoid issues with other insurance clauses, discuss with your broker and insurers how the policies may interact *before* a claim arises.

UNDERSTAND YOUR INSURANCE POLICIES

The importance of having a comprehensive understanding of your insurance policies can't be overstated. Make sure you have clarity around the following issues:

- Where are your manufacturing operations, and to what extent do your policies respond to natural disasters and geo-political/labor risks that may arise in such locations?

- Does your insurance cover damage to expensive equipment on your premises that could be damaged in the event of an explosion, overheating, mechanical breakdown, or other accident?

- How sophisticated are your supply chains, logistics, and distribution networks, and is your business interruption coverage protecting them?

- Where does the risk of losing any products in transit transfer from the seller to you, and does your cargo and stock throughput policy align with it?

- Do you produce goods that could be subject to a product recall (voluntary or involuntary) in the event of failure in the marketplace, and do you have appropriate coverage in place for such recalls if they occur?

- If your operations utilize chemicals or discharge any waste potentially having an impact on the environment, do you have coverage for any pollution you cause (or are alleged to have caused)?

- Does your cyber insurance policy adequately address the items we discussed in our earlier example?

- Do you have a board of directors, or other officers who require separate coverage for decisions they are making on behalf of your business?

- Are your operations located in an area with higher exposure to break-ins and theft?

- If you offer a 401(k) plan to you employees, does your insurance cover the fiduciaries (sponsors, administrators, advisors) responsible for bad decisions affecting the investments made by these employees?

- Have you entered into any contracts with third parties that require you to take on any insurance-related obligations?

- What exclusions exist in your policies that could disrupt the coverage you reasonably thought you had purchased?

- To what extent are your policies occurrence-based or claims-made, and what specific claim notification obligations do they trigger?

- Do you have overlapping coverage in more than one policy that could trigger sticky "other insurance" clauses?

This isn't an exhaustive list of the kinds of questions you need to answer about your insurance policies, but it can serve as a useful starting point. There may be many other questions you need to answer based on your specific business.

Practice proactive insurance management by identifying where you need coverage most along your Value Chain, and clarify *upfront* any vague, ambiguous, or confusing language in your insurance policies to avoid surprises. Test the insurer with hypothetical scenarios like the ones I've mentioned in this chapter, and see if you'd be covered. If so, get confirmation in writing, because you may need that "golden ticket" later. If not, determine how to secure that coverage, even if it means revisiting the market!

Understanding the nuances of your insurance policy can prevent scenarios like the one we're about to delve into, where a misunderstanding or oversight in policy terms led to unexpected coverage issues.

Case Study #2: Locker Room Talk

A certain company had, at times, exhibited a locker-room mentality. While not terribly overt, there had been a growing perception within the company that inappropriate and discriminatory comments were tolerated at certain levels of leadership. In fact, the Director of Human Resources had received a growing number of emails about the behavior of a certain VP of sales over the previous couple of years.

Company-wide training on appropriate workplace conduct had little apparent impact on this particular officer. One subordinate eventually had enough of the mistreatment and sued the company for harassment and discrimination, requesting a substantial damages award. Unfortunately for the company, they were located in an area renowned for pro-claimant and anti-company juries, and damage awards in the amount sought by this employee were not out of reach.

After dusting off the existing Employment Practices Liability Policy, the company noted that there was indeed coverage for harassment and discrimination claims, so they informed the insurer of the lawsuit. The insurer sent the company a response letter with the good news that they would be covering the claim, though subject to its standard reservation of rights (i.e., a list of provisions in the policy that could potentially trigger a reconsideration of coverage during the course of the claim).

The insurer then assigned a lawyer for the company to defend the lawsuit. This lawyer also reported back to the insurer on status and strategy items, which helped the insurer determine the appropriate amount of money to reserve for defense costs such as the attorney's fees, as well as losses in the event of settlement or verdict.

Several months into the lawsuit, which had largely been forgotten by some of the senior executives, the insurer sent a letter advising that they would no longer be covering the lawsuit. Remember what we said earlier about a "claims-made" policy, in which you're required to notify your insurer of a claim as a precondition to the insurer's obligation to cover it? Well, in this case, the insurer pointed out that the company had not provided notice of the claim within the same policy year that the claim was made, a necessary pre-condition to coverage.

In the policy, the insurer explained, a "claim" was defined as "a suit or demand made by a current, former, or prospective employee." The terms "suit" and "demand" were then further defined. A "suit" was defined to include traditional lawsuits and administrative claims such as EEOC charges. On the other hand, a "demand" was broadly defined to include "a request for monetary or non-monetary relief."

The insurer went on to explain that, during the discovery stage of the lawsuit, the plaintiff had requested and was provided with emails from the company demonstrating several instances of the VP's problematic conduct that had preceded the policy year. In at least two of these emails, employees had specifically threatened to sue the company if the conduct didn't improve, which the insurer was now interpreting to be "a request for non-monetary relief."

The company was blindsided by the fact that the insurer was now denying coverage on the grounds that the company's notice of the claim was late. As a result, they were left in the unenviable position of considering whether to spend significant sums suing the insurer, while simultaneously defending the employment lawsuit out-of-pocket.

Having read Chapters 3 and 4, you're probably thinking that this company should have had some form of policy governing harassment and discrimination in the workplace—and you'd be correct. The concepts of Preventive Law often work in tandem. Implementing such a policy might have avoided this scenario altogether. At a minimum, the company might have enjoyed reduced insurance premiums by having one.

The intricate dance between understanding your insurance policies and actively managing your business risks can't be underestimated.

This case study serves as a stark reminder that even with insurance in place, the lack of timely action and policy comprehension can lead to significant financial and reputational damage.

As you navigate through your business's insurance landscape, remember that insurance isn't just a safety net but a strategic tool. Use it wisely by staying informed, proactive, and prepared. Engage with your insurers, question ambiguities, and ensure your policies evolve with your business needs.

Only through diligent insurance management can you safeguard your business against unforeseen events, turning potential crises into mere bumps on the road to success!

Insurance Checklist

____ 120 days before purchasing or renewing insurance, set up an initial strategy meeting with a sophisticated broker to proactively determine the types and amounts of insurance that your business needs to carry.

____ Once you receive applications from the insurance company, spend plenty of time making sure they are complete and accurate.

____ 60 days before purchase/renewal, have your broker take your application to market.

____ 30 days before purchase/renewal, evaluate responses from insurance, sit down with your broker, and evaluate the best options.

____ Make sure to go over the policy thoroughly with your broker to ensure all necessary and expected coverage items are included.

continued…

___ Clarify any vague, ambiguous, or confusing language in your policy, looking for things like adequate limits and sub-limits, appropriate business interruption coverage, and contract exclusions, among other.

___ Review any potentially insurable losses during the prior policy year and make sure to discuss them with your broker or attorney to ensure they are reported to the insurer in a timely manner.

6

MANAGING CLAIMS & LAWSUITS

At some point, your business may find itself on the receiving end of a claim, or even a lawsuit. When that happens, don't despair. It's one of the risks of doing business.

Maybe you'll wind up defending yourself against a defective product claim, or a claim from a disgruntled employee. Or perhaps a commercial auto accident claim involving one of your drivers. It could be a contract dispute, an intellectual property claim, an environmental claim, union/labor trouble, or an antitrust investigation.

Whatever the case, your first course of action will probably be hiring a litigation attorney to represent your interests and letting them handle it. But hang on a minute. Don't simply hand the matter off to an attorney and wash your hands of the matter. You still need to be directly involved, managing your lawyer (or lawyers) and collaborating with them to understand and develop strategies that are business-forward.

In fact, you may even have the opportunity to settle that claim yourself before it ever turns into a lawsuit, which we'll discuss later. After all, this book is about steps you can take to sue-proof your business!

Speaking as a former litigator myself, and someone who has settled hundreds of claims and managed litigators in both insured and non-insured settings, I can't stress enough how important it is for a client company to remain directly involved in the claim and litigation process. I'll share an example.

AVOIDING A NIGHTMARE SCENARIO

Remember when I mentioned in the previous chapter that insurers and their counsel might not use litigation strategies that are in your best interest? Here's a perfect example of what this looks like.

A retail client of mine was one of several defendants who had been sued by the estate of an individual killed in an accident involving an alleged defect in a product they sold. Fortunately, the retailer was insured, so they forwarded the lawsuit to their insurance carrier, who assigned a lawyer to defend the company. Additionally, the retailer had an agreement with a third-party supplier that required the supplier to take full responsibility for defense and any damages from defect claims involving these products.

So far, so good. But a couple of months into the lawsuit, I was called by the CEO of the retailer after he had received a copy of a twenty-page status letter prepared by the lawyer assigned by the insurer. The language and legalese of the letter confused him. Since I had experience working with insurers and managing claims and lawsuits, he asked me to review the letter and provide guidance.

It didn't take long to realize there was a big problem. In the letter, the lawyer acknowledged the existence of the third-party supplier agreement, but they buried it low in a list of "to-do" action items. Instead, the lawyer recommended extensive discovery, with at least twenty to twenty-five depositions, retaining and deposing multiple experts, and then preparing and filing a couple of motions for good measure. To make matters worse, this lawyer claimed that the retailer could be found 15% – 25% liable for the death at trial, and that a jury verdict could well exceed $5 million.

Now, generally, when a lawsuit comes in, an insurance adjuster will estimate and set something called "defense cost reserves" based on the assigned lawyer's recommended strategy. This is money to be set aside by the insurer to pay for things like attorney fees, discovery costs, experts, and so on. The adjuster will also set "loss reserves" based on the anticipated settlement or trial value at different mile-markers in the case. To set the amount of these reserves, the adjuster largely relies on its assigned lawyer's periodic status letters.

In the retailer's case, a reasonable adjuster may have reviewed the lawyer's twenty-page letter and—based on the suggested strategy and exposure—set initial defense cost reserves of at least $50,000 with another $250,000 to $500,000 in loss reserves. This, of course, in addition to the $4,000-plus already spent in the initial review and preparation of that behemoth status letter.

Had the adjuster reserved in this way, the retailer's insurance premiums probably would have skyrocketed for the upcoming renewal period, despite the fact that this was their first claim related to an alleged product defect.

In other words, this twenty-page status letter was setting up a night-mare scenario for the retailer in terms of future costs. After reviewing the letter, I called the assigned lawyer and politely introduced myself as managing counsel for the case on behalf of the retailer, our mutual client.

We discussed the current strategy and realistic exposure assessment in light of the third-party supplier agreement, and I pointed to the indemnification language in the contract protecting the retailer. After I explained the unnecessary harm that could be done to the retailer at the insurance renewal, the lawyer agreed that the best course of action would be to instead immediately tender the defense (and all costs) over to the third-party supplier under the contract, performing only nec-essary discovery items in the interim. And in the event the supplier balked, we'd sue them and likely win since the contract language was crystal clear on this front.

Once we agreed to this new strategy, I requested the lawyer forward the insurance adjuster an updated status letter downgrading the anticipated loss exposure to a much lower nuisance-value settlement sum. All of this was set in motion within twenty-four hours of that phone call, and the case was then tendered to the third-party supplier to assume the defense of the retailer under the agreement.

To make this even more of a "happily ever after" situation, the supplier accepted our contract position without a fight and took over the defense. The case was settled at mediation with the retailer ultimately contributing nothing toward the settlement sum. At the following insurance renewal, the retailer's premium increased only a nominal amount as a result of the claim.

Now, don't get me wrong: an insurer's relationship with their assigned lawyer is important and necessary, because insurers need to be able to predict the outcomes of lawsuits in order to make business decisions for their clients (and themselves). However, if lawsuits are not also managed by an attorney who solely represents the insured business's interests, then there is a much higher chance that you're going to wind up with excessive defense costs, exposure to unnecessary strategies, and improper liability and damages assessments.

All of this can lead to skyrocketing premiums or worse: loss of insurance coverage altogether.

BEFORE YOU PUSH THE NUCLEAR BUTTON

So, what if the third-party supplier had refused to honor their contractual obligation to take full responsibility for the company's defense? As I said, we'd have considered (and likely would have) sued them. Sometimes, this is the wisest course of action, but suing someone is a bit like pushing the nuclear button. Before you do that, there are other steps you might want to take. Let's consider another scenario.

Let's suppose a strong storm passes through your area and does massive damage to your warehouse, creating significant business losses. You're confident that your losses will be covered by your commercial insurance policy. Considering how much money you spent on your premium at the last renewal, you think, "Boy, they'd *better* cover me!"

So you notify the insurance carrier and wait patiently for their investigation to be completed. But weeks go by, then a couple of months, and you don't get an answer from them.

Finally, you're fed up with the lack of response, so you announce, "I'm getting a lawyer, and I'm going after the insurance company! They've dragged their feet too long, and my warehouse is still damaged!"

You search for attorneys on Google, and you come across plenty of lawyers who are willing to help you get your money from the insurance company. Some are even willing to do it on a contingency basis, where they don't get paid unless you win damages. That seems like a good deal, and a great way to keep litigation costs to a bare minimum.

You finally retain the most aggressive-looking lawyer (at least based on the photos on the website), who then quickly whips off a demand letter and sends it to your insurer. The letter threatens a lawsuit, with bad faith claims, if insurance proceeds are not received within thirty days. Well, the insurer defiantly ignores the letter, so on the morning of day thirty-one, your attorney files a lawsuit seeking everything but the kitchen sink, including punitive damages to make an example out of that no-good insurer.

It seems like a smart approach. Just the possibility of being hit with punitive damages should cause the insurer to curl up on the floor in a fetal position. And then they'll surely pay up!

"Eeeeexcellent," you mutter, in your best villain voice. It's only a matter of time now!

But as it turns out, litigation meanders its way through the court system for two miserable years, and in the end, the judge sides with the insurer. You lose the lawsuit, and you end up paying to fix your warehouse out of your own pocket.

Instead, if you'd taken advantage of pre-lawsuit opportunities, you might have been able to resolve the claim amicably and to your general satisfaction, but that can't happen now. You pushed the nuclear button, and your relationship with your insurer blew up!

Here are some things you should have done before hiring an attorney:

1) WTF Is A-OK

First and foremost, consider the possibility that there is a reasonable excuse for the insurer's delay. Every year, property insurers face massive exposure due to natural disasters occurring across the country, from hurricanes to tornadoes to wildfires. Resources (including claims adjusters) must be triaged and deployed to the biggest losses at the expense of smaller claims (comparatively speaking).

Still, it's perfectly acceptable to ask the insurer, "WTF?" (or more diplomatic words to that effect). Even better, hire a lawyer to assist you with resolving your claim amicably (as a professionally-worded "WTF?"). This typically results in quicker engagement by the adjuster.

Above all, patience, thoughtful strategy, and a focus on the ultimate goal (i.e., maximizing insurance recoveries) should *always* take precedence over hastily taking the insurer to court.

Once you start making aggressive overtures and threats, it's far more likely that the claims handler will simply hand the matter over to their legal department. This is especially true when you start using the nuclear phrase "bad faith," and even more so when that phrase is uttered by your lawyer. Look, there's a time and place for hostility, but not until after you've exhausted every amicable pathway available— and only if you have a solid basis for asserting such a claim. Now isn't the time to lose your credibility.

Also, the insurer's coverage lawyer may be more inclined to deny coverage outright than the previous claims adjuster. I know this because I *was* a coverage lawyer inside an insurance company at one time.

2) For Whom the Bell "Tolls"

While you're working on your patience, keep in mind there's a statute of limitations that effectively bars any lawsuit filed after a certain deadline. These statutes vary by state and by the nature of the claim being asserted (e.g., contract vs. tort). To add to the frustration, your insurance policy may further limit such deadlines. In fact, many policies require a lawsuit against the insurer to be filed within *one year* of the inception of loss. That one-year period could begin on the date of the event of loss itself, not the date you discovered the loss.

Therefore, if your insurer's delay is pushing you close to a deadline, make sure to ask them for something called a "tolling agreement," which will temporarily extend the statute of limitations while the parties amicably attempt to resolve the claim. You shouldn't have any problem getting this agreement. Whatever you do, don't wait until after the deadline passes to take action, because then you're sunk! Your attorney should be well-versed in tolling agreements and able to negotiate these with the insurer.

Once you have a tolling agreement in place, spend some time learning more about the insurer's investigation, reasonably cooperating with them as required under the insurance policy. Also, research similar cases which might be favorable (or adverse) to your position and evaluate the respective merits of each other's positions.

Again, don't be quick to go on the offensive, but definitely don't concede any insurer positions that could have negative consequences later, especially in writing (those will likely become exhibits if a lawsuit is filed). You should also review and consider potential litigation strategies and outcomes—just don't let your insurer know you're doing so.

3) By Failing to Prepare, You Prepare to Fail

At some point, you'll get the insurer's final settlement position. Armed with this information, consider the following:

- Is the insurer willing to pay something now? If so, how much?

- How much will it cost to sue the insurer (in terms of attorney fees and court costs) through the different stages of litigation (e.g., motion to dismiss, motion for summary judgment, trial, appeal)?

- What are the chances you could lose at each stage?

- What are the chances you could win, including your chances of prevailing without even having to go to trial (e.g., a summary judgment motion)?

- Assuming you win, what's the likely amount of recovery? Bear in mind, you're more likely to win contract damages than bad faith tort damages.

Also, consider the drain on your management's time and resources, especially during the arduous discovery stage, when both parties are gathering and exchanging information and evidence. And consider the risk of developing a reputation as a "litigious insured," which may burn bridges with insurers who tag you as a problematic risk.

Evaluate all of these issues and weigh them against the settlement opportunity in front of you—that's sound business decision-making. It's certainly less risky than hastily pushing that nuclear "lawsuit" button and then hoping you're not within the fallout radius. And at the end of your analysis, you may find that the insurer has already offered you the best-case scenario outcome, all things considered.

Assigned Lawyers Aren't the Only Lawyers You Should Manage

As I said, it's important to remain directly involved, managing your litigation attorneys, and this applies to more than insurance cases. We had a product client with factories in multiple states who had a lot of union employees. Their relationship with the union became strained over a couple of years, with the union filing numerous unfair labor practice charges, largely to prove a point.

The company simply handed these claims over to their long-time law firm to defend without any oversight. After two years of unmanaged litigation, the firm had racked up nearly $300,000 in legal fees, even as they unilaterally increased their rates and made a bunch of questionable staffing and strategy choices. The senior partner finally recommended taking the union dispute through trial and appeals, despite the low probability of success. This would have forced the company to spend several hundred thousand dollars in additional fees to the firm. And to make matters even more horrible, the trial date was set in less than thirty days!

Fortunately, the company recognized the huge risk, so they hired my law practice to take a look at the case. We immediately interviewed their long-term lawyers to try to make sense of their ongoing litigation strategy. To our astonishment, we discovered that these issues were just the tip of the iceberg! Among other things, we learned that there had been multiple opportunities to settle with the union at a fraction of what the company had already spent in legal fees. The law firm had also failed to realize that there was insurance coverage available to offset some of the company's losses.

It became clear that the law firm was not protecting the company's best interests, so we quickly replaced them with a more business-forward firm. Then we collaborated closely with the new attorneys to pivot away from trial strategy and toward settlement discussions. In the meantime, we notified the client's insurance carrier of a provision in the policy that allowed coverage for a portion of the fees and settlement given the nature of the claims being made by the union.

In the end, we successfully settled the pending labor charges for a fraction of what would have been spent litigating, and over half of the sum was reimbursed by insurance. We then helped the company rebuild their relationship with the union and restore trust so they could collaborate on developing internal policies that would minimize the likelihood of this kind of legal circus happening again. Within a few months, the relationship had improved to a point where disputes were being handled amicably without any threat of lawsuits.

That's what proactive litigation management looks like. It's all about understanding the strategies being considered by counsel throughout each stage of a lawsuit, as well as their consequences to your business, and then working directly with counsel to fine-tune and implement them.

Spending $150,000 on attorneys' fees to go through litigation may not make business sense when you have an opportunity to settle early on for $100,000. On the other hand, taking a couple of defensible product claims through trial may send a message to prospective claimants to think twice when deciding whether they should go after your business—thus minimizing the number of future claims and future premium exposure.

By navigating these situations wisely, you not only manage the immediate financial implications but also set a precedent for how your business handles adversity. This approach can significantly reduce the number of future claims and, consequently, keep your future premium exposure in check.

Now, speaking of managing future headaches, let's dive into something equally critical yet often overlooked until it's too late: the importance of retaining evidence. You see, in the legal labyrinth, evidence isn't just king; it's the entire kingdom. Here's why you need to care about every scrap of paper and byte of data.

THE IMPORTANCE OF RETAINING EVIDENCE

Important note: the target of any claim or lawsuit is required to retain *all* material evidence. This requirement includes the period of time *before* litigation, when a party should reasonably know that evidence may be relevant to possible litigation. Failure to do so can lead to significant court sanctions, including monetary penalties and even an instruction to a jury that they can infer from your destruction of evidence that it contained information harmful to your case.

This is why you need to develop and implement a **Record Retention Policy**. A record retention policy governs how long you retain various categories of documents across your enterprise, and further identifies appropriate and mandated protocols in the event of litigation or when the threat of investigation, claim, or litigation first arises.

What to Include in Your Record Retention Policy

A good record retention policy governs the creation, retention, and destruction of all company business records. It includes guidelines for how long certain documents should be kept and how records should be destroyed.

The policy should generally begin by identifying the purpose of effective records management, such as better organization and decision-making; maximizing available workspace; business continuity in the event of a catastrophic event; prompt response to investigations, claims, and litigation; and compliance with all federal, state, and even international legal and regulatory requirements.

After that, the policy should state that compliance with the policy is mandatory, and it should list the consequences for failing to do so. A good policy should also list the types of documents and information that will be covered, which will probably include the final forms of communications, data, and recordings of information listed in the attached schedule (which we will discuss shortly).

And then it should list the documents and information that will *not* be covered, such as:

1. Unannotated duplicates

2. Preliminary drafts of certain documents that don't reference significant decision-making

3. Texts

4. Spam, junk mail, or materials originating outside the business

5. Certain private materials involving personal affairs

Handling of both hard copy and electronic records should be addressed, with a focus on the latter since electronic records can take many forms and may be found in numerous storage media. You want to emphasize the importance to employees of not casually destroying electronically-stored information, so the term "Electronic Data" in your record retention policy may be defined broadly to include "all text files, spreadsheets, emails, voicemails, recorded conversations, databases, calendar and scheduling information, data generated by calendaring, task and personal information management, computer system activity logs, electronic control modules (ECMs), electronic data records (EDRs), GPS tracking devices, and all file fragments and backup files containing Electronic Data."

Of course, this requirement shouldn't be limited to individual employees. It also applies to anyone responsible for managing electronically stored information (ESI) interfaces, such as your IT representatives.

Often, to maintain system space, default rules are implemented that automatically destroy business emails from Inbox, Sent, and Deleted folders after a certain period of time (typically two years). That could be a problem. Many of those emails may constitute records that need to be maintained if some triggering event occurs, so your policy needs to demand prompt response.

To avoid any confusion, "triggering events" should be listed in some detail in the policy. What's a triggering event? Typically, any investigation, claim, or litigation. As we already mentioned, your record retention obligations generally begin when you should have reasonably anticipated such an event, not necessarily when it was actually filed or served.

Ultimately, your policy should conclude with a robust schedule of all departments where subject records can be found, all categories of documents, the responsible record holder or manager, the retention period for each category of documents, and the reason for such retention period.

Yes, I know, all of this sounds incredibly complex, and it is. There's no getting around it. Identifying and shepherding the development and implementation of a record retention policy can get incredibly complicated, so consider working with a records retention attorney or specialist actively involved in the initial process and subsequent refreshers. If you have the means to create an internal records management team, make sure it consists of diverse stakeholders within the business, including C-suite leaders, to ensure appropriate visibility and accountability.

Record Retention Policy Checklist

___ Identify the purpose of effective records management.

___ State that compliance is mandatory and list the consequences for failing to comply.

___ List the types of documents and information that will (and will not) be covered.

___ Address the handling of both hard copy and electronic records, with a focus on electronic records.

___ Conclude with a list of:

    ___ All departments where subject records can be found

    ___ All categories of documents

continued...

___ The responsible record holders

___ The retention period for each category of documents

___ The reason for such a retention period

The Hold Order

Once you have a "reasonable anticipation" that an investigation, claim, or lawsuit might occur, you're legally required to institute a "Hold Order" in accordance with your record retention policy. This Hold Order will direct certain individuals to suspend the destruction policy in regard to certain kinds of documents related to the triggering event that may be in their possession—and will further explain the specific reasons for the suspension.

A Hold Order should define the timeframe during which these documents need to be preserved, with both a start date and an anticipated end date, or a range of dates, and it should clarify if this will apply to future documents (which is known as an "Evergreen Hold"). With an Evergreen Hold, the order should provide instructions on how to perform the creation and retention of future documents on an ongoing basis.

Make sure the Hold Order is neither under-inclusive nor over-inclusive in scope. Rather, it should define the specific issues in dispute and the issues related to any claims or defenses. If the Hold Order pertains to a lawsuit that has been filed, then the lawsuit should be mentioned by name.

The order should describe the types of documents that need to be preserved without attempting to list every possible data source. For example, it might say something like, "Among other documents, this includes handwritten notes, emails, and other electronic documents."

The instructions should further state that a failure to comply may result in civil or criminal penalties for the company or, in cases of willful noncompliance, for the individual. Your record retention policy should already list disciplinary measures for failure to comply, and that includes Hold Orders.

So who should receive the Hold Order, and who is responsible for carrying it out? Again, avoid being too under-inclusive or over-inclusive. Instead, consider a few key targets for the hold. Relevant IT staff should certainly be part of the preservation process due to their data expertise. Make sure to stop any regularly-scheduled deletion of emails from these key players.

Bear in mind, if an investigation, claim, or lawsuit does happen, you may be required to produce your record retention policy to prove that you aren't destroying relevant and material evidence for the proceedings. That being said, you probably shouldn't produce the Hold Order itself or the list of employees receiving it. Instead, I always recommend that the Hold Order come from your company's legal department (if you have one) or an outside lawyer as part of a confidential and privileged attorney-client communication containing the specific advice and instructions.

Once the investigation, claim, or lawsuit has concluded and your record retention policy can be resumed, forward a "Release of Hold Order" to your recipient list to let them know.

ABOUT THAT ATTORNEY-CLIENT PRIVILEGE

Attorney-client privilege can be a powerful tool for keeping nosy outsiders from accessing sensitive emails, letters, phone calls, and other types of private communications and discussions. This legal principle ensures that your company is able to seek and obtain confidential legal advice about sensitive issues without fear of those discussions being shared with unfriendly parties, particularly if there's an investigation, claim, or lawsuit.

However, just bringing your attorney into a business meeting or copying them on a particular email does not automatically trigger the application of this privilege—neither does adding the words "Confidential Attorney-Client Discussion" at the top of a document. In fact, there are some discussions that you or your employees may have with a lawyer that are not covered by attorney-client privilege.

So, when does it apply? Here is the basic rule of thumb:

First, to invoke attorney-client privilege, the communication with your lawyer must involve the giving and receiving of legal advice and strategy. In other words, if you're communicating with the lawyer solely to get *business* advice or strategy, it likely will *not* be protected.

What about correspondence that blurs the line between business and legal strategy items? If an adverse party seeks that correspondence in the course of a lawsuit and files a motion with a court compelling you to produce it, then a judge will ultimately decide if the privilege applies. If you're in a jurisdiction that is unfavorable to your business, this may be a problem.

Second, to invoke attorney-client privilege, the discussion must involve a communication that takes place *exclusively* between your company's representatives and your lawyer. If an otherwise-privileged discussion is shared with a non-company third party, or if a third party is present at the time of the discussion, the privilege will be broken for that discussion.

For example, let's say you're contemplating a lawsuit against your insurance company for denying a claim that you believe should have been covered under the terms of the policy. You have an internal strategy meeting with your lawyer and key employees to discuss the relative strengths and weaknesses of your legal arguments, as well as likely outcomes in a court of law. All of this discussion is incorporated into a legal memorandum and circulated to the team for review and further comment (with "Confidential Attorney-Client Discussion" prominently displayed at the top).

What if your company's insurance manager is present for the discussion, and she decides to forward the memorandum to the company's insurance broker for additional review and comment? Unfortunately, doing so may break the privileged in certain states, and you'd now be required to produce the memorandum during the course of litigation.

Finally, be aware that if you break the attorney-client privilege in one specific discussion or correspondence, a judge may decide that you've waived the privilege when it comes to other discussions involving the same or similar discussions—even if those other discussions would have otherwise been considered privileged.

Don't give opposing attorneys the opportunity to make those arguments in court. Be cautious and proactive about involving your business lawyer in discussions, and even more cautious about how you document those discussions!

THE DANGERS OF NOT PLAYING NICE

Let's suppose you're a snack manufacturer of a popcorn-based snack product. You operate a fleet of trucks for transporting your products to distribution warehouses. During one such trip, one of your drivers rear-ends a small hybrid vehicle, which she claims suddenly pulled into her lane. Police prepare a statement that indicates your driver was at fault, but a review of the dashcam footage (most insurance companies now require dashcams as a precondition of insuring commercial fleets) shows that the accident was not entirely her fault. Indeed, the fault may be split 50/50.

Your company then receives a call from the hybrid owner requesting payment for his vehicle damage in the amount of $9,000. He hasn't made any claim for pain or suffering related to the accident; he just wants the repairs paid so he doesn't have to submit his claim to his insurance company.

You respond that the dashcam footage shows your driver was not totally at fault, but you still agree to offer the hybrid driver a sum of $5,000, over half the cost of repairs. He refuses your offer and threatens to get an attorney involved if the total repair estimate isn't paid in full.

So, what do you do?

Looking into the crystal ball and considering potential scenarios (including worst-case scenarios) may help guide your strategy.

Let's say you refuse to pay the total repair estimate, and the claimant winds up retaining an attorney. After mysteriously developing neck pain symptoms following the initial visit with the lawyer, the claimant is sent by his lawyer to see a physician, who in turn sends the claimant for X-rays and an MRI. Surprise, surprise, the physician finds evidence of age-related disc degeneration in the cervical spine.

The physician then writes up a report for the lawyer stating that the claimant's current "severe" pain is the result of an aggravation of his pre-existing disc degeneration, directly caused by the accident with your driver. As a result, the physician recommends a course of physical therapy followed by referral to an orthopedic surgeon to discuss the possibility of multi-level cervical fusion surgery.

The orthopedic surgeon does in fact recommend this surgery, and the procedure is performed a few weeks later, followed by several follow-up medical appointments and therapy. A few months after you triumphantly told the claimant to pound sand on the $9,000 repair bill, you receive a threatening letter from the claimant's lawyer with several medical bills and reports enclosed totaling over $50,000 in medical costs, which the physician claims were a direct result of the accident. The police report, which said your driver was at fault, is also included.

Finally, there's a letter from the claimant's lawyer demanding that you pay $300,000 in total to settle this claim. Otherwise, they are going to file a lawsuit.

There's no way you're going to pay such a ridiculous claim, so you submit it to your insurer. The insurer assigns a lawyer to defend your interests as well as theirs. However, after your insurer spends close to $40,000 in defense and expert costs, as well as the assigned lawyer's fees, they make the strategic decision to settle the case at mediation for $150,000 due to the risks of putting this case in front of a jury at a trial.

Following settlement, your insurer sends you an invoice to pay the $25,000 deductible in connection with the lawsuit (or whatever deductible you chose—hopefully it wasn't too high).

To make matters worse, at your next insurance renewal, your commercial auto insurance premium is increased substantially as a result of this lawsuit, which cost your insurer over $190,000 (minus the deductible). Until then, you had a spotless loss history, but your record is now compromised.

A rather horrible outcome to this whole legal mess.

But It Didn't Have to Go That Way

What could you have done differently? Well, you could have agreed to pay the claimant the extra $4,000 in repair estimates, and then forwarded a waiver and release of liability form for the claimant to sign and return before getting the check. This form—which you should already have prepared as part of your standard contract forms package for deployment in scenarios like this—includes a release of all claims in connection with the accident, including claims for bodily injury.

Is there a possibility the claimant will just pocket the check and never get the repairs? Of course, but that's not your problem. Stay focused on proactively minimizing your exposure to legal risks—and this is most certainly a risk. Your driver had *some* level of fault (between 50% and 100%), so your company certainly bears *some* responsibility. But the annoyance of having to pay $9,000 total in total repair costs should be greatly outweighed by the much greater annoyance of having to pay tens of thousands more by refusing to do so.

So what happens if you receive the signed release and pay the $9,000, only for the claimant to later decide he's going to retain a lawyer and send you a threatening letter anyway? Well, if that happens, you simply send a professional response letter or email to his lawyer explaining that the claimant already released any such claim. Perhaps you even include a copy of the signed release form.

Chances are, the claimant hasn't told his lawyer about the signed release form, so when his lawyer sees that document, they're probably going to fire the claimant as a client and go away.

When Fighting Back Is the Best Option

I can't speak for you, but between these two options, I'd prefer the second one. As a business owner, it would be far less painful. Nevertheless, there are certain times when taking a client to court makes more sense. Consider the following scenario involving a different type of claim.

In Chapter 2, we used an example of a customer who claimed she broke a tooth on a piece of plastic hidden in a snack food box. Now, the customer claims she had to get dental implants to fix her broken tooth, and she's demanding a $50,000 payment from your snack food company in reimbursement for the implants plus her pain and suffering.

You conduct an investigation and discover that there is no real proof that your snack product caused the damage, just the customer's testimony. It's entirely possible that your product had nothing to do with it. Furthermore, the claimant admits that she didn't save the alleged piece of plastic, nor did she take any pictures of it. She also failed to take any pictures of the broken tooth.

You instruct your quality assurance team to pull batch records from that particular production run, and you find no evidence whatsoever of any problems that might have put a piece of plastic in that box. So how are you supposed to respond to the customer's claim?

Clearly, the claim seems far more suspicious than the auto accident claim in our previous story. In fact, negotiating and paying out a claim like this could open up a Pandora's Box of claimants accusing your company of all kinds of nefarious deeds. Why? Because people now know that you'll pay claims without proof.

In a situation like this, you're far better off telling the claimant to pound sand. Don't say that literally, of course. An aggressive position or hostile words can make their way to the general public via social media and damage your reputation and goodwill.

Instead, to avoid any business blowback in dealing with customer claims like this, consider engaging a well-respected third-party administrator service (TPA) to perform the claim investigation and negotiation services for your business. TPA services have the tools and data points to determine your likely exposure to specific claims and will run interference for you, pushing back on customers to provide evidence supporting their claims.

Following investigation, if the TPA obtains sufficient evidence to support the customer's claim, they may recommend that you settle and give the TPA authorization to do so (subject to a signed release). However, if no evidence is found to support the claim, the TPA will let you know and may further request the opportunity to negotiate that claimant's bottom line.

There's no harm in negotiating at this point, especially through your TPA. In fact, you may learn that the dental implant surgery was covered by the claimant's insurance, and that the claimant is really only looking for payment of the $1,000 deductible. That's a significant enough drop from the initial $50,000 claim that it may make good business sense to pay the $1,000 in exchange for a signed release.

However, if the claimant stands firm on her $50,000 demand, your TPA can deny the claim for you in a professional manner, then sit back and wait to see if any lawyers are willing to represent a client with no real evidence.

Managing Claims & Lawsuits Checklist

___ When dealing with a business loss, if your insurance company doesn't respond to your claim in a timely manner, do the following things before considering litigation:

    ___ Be patient!

    ___ Request a tolling agreement to avoid any deadlines or statute of limitations.

    ___ Cooperate with the insurer's investigation, but don't concede any position that could have adverse consequences later.

    ___ When you get the insurer's final settlement position, evaluate it carefully and weigh the risks of litigating.

___ Proactively manage your litigation attorneys to make sure their strategies align with your business goals.

    ___ Consider retaining legal counsel to manage attorneys assigned by the insurer, or as a sounding board in non-insurance settings.

___ Develop and implement robust a Record Retention Policy.

    ___ In the event of an investigation, claim, or lawsuit might occur, institute a Hold Order.

___ Remember, attorney-client privilege only applies to communications in which you are receiving legal advice and strategy. Third parties should not be present, and discussions related to business strategies within those communications may be excepted from the privilege.

continued...

___ Make business decisions in deciding whether to settle claims early, balancing things like:

   ___ Costs of settling early versus litigating through trial

   ___ Perception in marketplace by fighting against your customers

   ___ Sending a message that you stand by your products or services and are not afraid to defend them

___ Consider using a TPA to help you investigate, negotiate, and settle these claims on your behalf.

7

DUE DILIGENCE

Before buying a new or used vehicle, a smart shopper will usually say something like, "I'm just gonna peek under the hood." Why? Because they want to make sure they're not buying a lemon, and that requires rolling up your sleeves and doing some hands-on research before signing on the dotted line.

The same approach applies to any business making a significant purchase.

Let's suppose your company has grown to the point where you're considering acquiring a competitor's business. First, let me congratulate you on your enormous success. Now, to ensure it *remains* a success, you need to proactively conduct due diligence before you close the transaction.

What's due diligence? In this case, it's an in-depth review, analysis, and evaluation of the target business to make sure there are no red flags that might come back to bite you—just like looking under the hood of the car to make sure you're not buying a lemon.

MAKE A LIST, CHECK IT TWICE

To keep your due diligence process focused and organized, first create a checklist of information and documents that you need to request from the other side. Don't inundate them with a twenty-page list of items—that's counterproductive—unless you're looking at a major, large-scale acquisition or merger. Instead, start with the broad strokes of what you need, and then narrow your focus on any red flag items you uncover along the way.

Since you're probably going to be dealing with a lot of sensitive business, financial, marketing, and intellectual property information and material in these documents, you'll likely need to negotiate and sign some form of NDA. If you're also going to be providing your own confidential information and documents as part of the evaluation, make sure the agreement is mutual.

Here are some of the documents you need to request:

1) Formation & Governance Documents

Begin by requesting their formation and governance documents. If the target business hasn't followed appropriate formalities here, it's a huge red flag. As we discussed in Chapter 1, after setting up a business entity, all business owners are required to proactively govern that entity from initial documentation all the way through growth and global domination.

Depending on the type of entity, and the number of business owners, they should have some bylaws or agreement governing the actions of the owners, as well as minutes, consents, and resolutions that tell the history of the business. Make sure all of these documents exist! You don't want to be blindsided by compliance landmines or exposure from a current or potential owner who could disrupt the acquisition or merger after closing.

Consider the following governing documents as a starting point:

- **Formation & Governance Documents**

    → Certificate of Incorporation/Organization

→ Good Standing Certificate

→ Bylaws/Operating Agreements

→ Minutes

→ Consents/Resolutions

→ Buy-Sell Agreements

→ Warrant/Option Agreements (which may entitle certain beneficiaries to purchase ownership at a fixed price)

2) Financials

It goes without saying that your target business's financial performance is important. Don't rely on what they tell you. Instead, get copies of records you can review yourself to determine their performance. A single year of prior records isn't enough. You need to go further back to track any trends. I recommend asking for up to five years of returns and financial statements—that isn't an unreasonable request.

Consider hiring an experienced accountant or other financial expert to provide guidance about any pitfalls that might exist in the financial records.

Your initial checklist should look something like this:

- **Financials**

    → Tax returns (federal/state, last 5 years, including any sale and use tax returns)

    → Financial statements (last 5 years)

    → Tax liens (if any)

→ Uniform Commercial Code (UCC) liens (if any)

3) Agreements

A company's contracts and agreements with third parties are the life-blood of its business, and they may be the primary reason you're so interested in acquiring this particular business. However, you'll want to review these agreements to make sure you're not going to take on any burdensome, impossible, or impractical obligations. You also need to find out if any one-sided language exists that might limit your opportunities to recover damages in the event of a default or breach by a prospective contractual counterpart.

In addition to their business contracts, you'll also want to review agreements related to your target business's premises, particularly if you'll be assuming lease obligations with an existing landlord—or instead acquiring the real estate and therefore assuming obligations with existing tenants—as part of the overall transaction.

Finally, you need to know if your target business has been appropriately insured.

The agreements section of your checklist might look something similar to this:

- **Agreements**
    - → Business Contracts
        - ◦ Vendor, distributor, customer agreements
        - ◦ Intellectual property agreements
        - ◦ Equipment leases
    - → Real Estate

- ◦ Leases

- ◦ Purchase agreements/deeds

- ◦ Surveys/environmental studies

- ◦ Title insurance policies

- ◦ Identity of any consents required for acquisition/ merger

- ◦ Rent liabilities

→ Insurance

- ◦ All policies of insurance

4) Licenses & Permits

Next, depending on the industry involved, your target business may require certain federal, state, or municipal licenses or permits. Make sure they are appropriately licensed and permitted and that they are current.

The checklist for licenses and permits should look like this:

- **Licenses & Permits**

  → Federal

  → State

  → Municipalities

  → Others

5) Assets

Your target business's contracts are not the only shiny things attracting you to this acquisition. You may also be interested in their assets. Make sure to request a list of information and documents related to these assets so you can confirm that you'll actually be receiving what you expect to receive in this transaction:

- **Assets**

    → Cash

    → Securities

    → Equipment

    → Inventory

    → Intellectual Property

      ◦ Patents (issued and pending)

      ◦ Trademarks

      ◦ Copyrights

      ◦ Trade secrets

      ◦ Domain names

      ◦ Other proprietary rights

6) Liabilities

What would assets be without liabilities? Naturally, this will be the next section you want to investigate. Check to see if there are any obligations, claims, lawsuits, or investigations that could blindside you. These are often deal-breakers, so you'll want to identify them early:

- **Liabilities**

    → Bank debt

    → Threatened, pending, and current lawsuits

    → Claims asserted and reported to insurance carriers

    → Licensing violations

    → Government investigations

7) Employment

Now, let's return to their business practices and learn about the people who work for them. Request information on how many people your target business employs, their cost of employment, and which employees are critical during a transition period and for continued operation (in case you're considering "synergies" or downsizing immediately after closing).

Get copies of your target business's internal employment policies and practices, including the employee handbook and any specific work-related policies that are not included in the handbook. These may be more relevant when acquiring (or merging with) a manufacturing business with production lines.

The employee section of your due diligence checklist might initially look like this:

- **Employment**

    → Number of employees

→ List of employees and officers (with current titles and salaries)

→ Identities of employees key to the successful transition and continued operation of business

→ Copy of employee handbook

→ Copies of work-related policies

→ Bonuses earned and not yet paid

→ Employee benefits

  ◦ Insurance

  ◦ Pension

  ◦ 401(k)

  ◦ Bonuses

8) Negative Publicity

Last, brand and goodwill are also important considerations in your acquisition or merger, particularly if the target business is a product manufacturer. Request information related to any customer problems or negative publicity they've had in the past:

• **Negative Publicity / Customer Problems (if any)**

Bear in mind, the items I've listed in the previous section are just a starting point. The particulars of your industry may necessitate beefing up one or more of these sections, or even adding additional sections. For example, if you're acquiring a medical device company, you'll want to know the extent of any market corrective actions or product recalls.

In that case, you might expand the "Negative Publicity" and "Liabilities" sections to include specific requests for these regulatory actions and recalls. You might also add a new section within your target business's regulatory practices to investigate compliance on that front.

As documents start rolling in, you can decide whether you have enough information to satisfy your concerns about specific subjects. And if red flags emerge, request supplemental information and documents until you get the answers you need. Your ultimate goal is to make an informed business decision related to your target business— so get the information you need to do so!

THIS COULD HAPPEN TO YOU

The due diligence process shouldn't be taken lightly. Any failure to uncover or address landmines within your target business can create huge problems for you down the road. Consider the following possible scenarios involving a prospective acquisition target:

- They have a shareholder who owns a significant percentage of the company but is conspicuously absent from company minutes, consents, and resolutions involving key decisions.

- They have operations in several states, but they've failed to appropriately register to do business in half of them.

- They recently received a demand letter from a lawyer regarding a potential class action involving a product defect.

- They have received several letters from local and state environmental agencies regarding an overflow of hazardous waste into a nearby river.

- They have a significant union presence, and the local union has filed several recent unfair labor practice charges against the company.

- They sell products primarily through direct-to-consumer channels but have not implemented appropriate cybersecurity measures, including procuring cyber insurance.

- Their land and equipment are largely tied up by third-party lenders, with additional judgment liens filed in the local recorder's office.

- They have a long-standing relationship with an overseas factory that is notorious for harsh employee conditions.

These are just a small number of potential issues you could uncover during the due diligence process. You'll want to learn more about them before deciding whether or not to proceed with closing. Whatever the case, having a robust checklist—and then following up with additional requests based on what you find—ensures that no stone is left unturned.

Here is a real-life case study that demonstrates the importance of proactive due diligence in mergers and acquisitions:

Case Study #1: Mystery Shells

A product manufacturer engaged us to assist with a prospective acquisition. During the initial interview, the Chief Financial Officer informed us that her company was in the process of negotiating several significant global business opportunities and realized that a major infusion of capital was needed to accommodate these opportunities. She made it clear that venture capital was not an option, and an initial public offering would be too costly and time-consuming. I then learned that she had been working with a facilitator over several weeks to quickly raise capital through a reverse merger.

A reverse merger involves an active company merging with a defunct company that only exists on paper (also known as a "shell company"). Since these shell companies have already gone through all the necessary steps to trade publicly, they can be attractive to companies seeking to avoid the onerous time and cost commitments of going through these steps themselves.

During that meeting, I had the following exchange with the CFO:

> CFO: "Chris, is this merger something you'd be willing to help us with?"
>
> Me: "Sure, but I'll need to know a little more about the facilitator and the shell company."
>
> CFO: "Okay, but we're good with them on our end. We really just need you to prepare the merger agreements so we can close on this deal."
>
> Me: "Whoa, let's take a step back. What specific due diligence have you done on them?"
>
> CFO: "The facilitator is a long-time friend and neighbor of mine. He said the shell is a perfect fit for our business and this should be a simple deal. I trust him."
>
> Me: "So you haven't done *any* due diligence of your own?"
>
> CFO: "No, not really."

I explained to the CFO that there are reasons why shell companies are defunct, so conducting extensive diligence on them is incredibly important, regardless of who the facilitator is. Some shell companies have been used to defraud federal regulators, making them dangerous vehicles for raising capital.

After a bit more back and forth, the CFO finally agreed to conduct due diligence to uncover any potential red flags before taking the next step—even though this would cause a delay in closing. The last thing she wanted was a knock on the door from federal investigators after completing the merger.

First, we created a robust checklist of documents that she needed to request from the shell company's owner, including all business and tax records. We also researched public filings and litigation histories involving the owner and facilitator.

Through this initial process, we learned that the shell company had begun as a publicly-traded arts and crafts business. After going out of business, the original owners presented it to the public as a shell company, which was then acquired by the current owner through another reverse merger. The new owner then presented the shell company to the public as an energy exporting business (and not a shell).

This is where things got really interesting (and messy).

Despite having removed the "shell" designation from its public filings, this energy exporting company had prepared no financial statements and listed no revenues for any of the years during which they operated. However, they listed the same amount of nominal costs each year—$2,500 in "professional" fees—all of which were paid to the owner. The owner also appeared to have interests in several other shell companies that he claimed were based out of Nevada and Utah. All of those companies involved mining and energy activities, though none of them had any real operations.

Of course, this created quite a few red flags from our perspective. We saw potential catastrophe looming on the horizon for our client.

In an effort to get some clarification, we held a conference call with the owner of the shell company and the facilitator. The owner persisted in his claim that the alleged exporting company had operated for several years, but he was curiously unable to explain the lack of revenues, or the "professional fees" paid to himself. When we asked about his other shell companies, he sheepishly admitted his involvement, noting over twenty shell-related deals with the facilitator. The facilitator acknowledged the existence of this prior relationship, much to the surprise of our client CFO.

After a few more follow-up questions, and some less-than-satisfactory responses from the owner and facilitator, I asked what percentage of the outstanding shares had been sold after the shell company began presenting itself as an exporting business. My concern was that the owner had been fraudulently raising capital by selling shares in a business that wasn't actually operating. The owner was adamant that the number of shares sold was zero.

Fortunately, I'd already received a shareholder list from a third-party investigative firm that showed the number to be closer to 98%. I revealed this to the owner and attempted to probe further into how these funds were raised and used by the company, since that information wasn't in any of the documents they provided. At that moment, the owner suddenly dropped off the call, never to be heard from again, and the facilitator quickly followed suit.

The frustrated CFO ultimately conceded that the significant legal and business risks uncovered during the due diligence process warranted walking away from this deal—and away from the overall strategy of raising capital through a reverse merger. Although she was discouraged to be back at square one, she was glad to have avoided exposing her business to civil and criminal sanctions.

This rigorous approach to due diligence doesn't stop at business acquisitions or mergers; it's equally critical when dealing with real estate. Whether you're expanding your business operations, investing in property, or even considering real estate as part of a larger business deal, the principles of due diligence remain paramount.

REAL ESTATE DUE DILIGENCE

It should be clear by now that thorough due diligence needs to be your standard protocol when you're considering an acquisition or merger. However, it's just as important to perform the same level of research on any prospective business real estate purchase prior to closing. Consider the following case study:

Case Study #2: Hidden Environmental Conditions

When a national manufacturer was looking to establish a presence in another area of the country, the CEO came to us for assistance to assist with investigation prior to closing. The company was under contract for a large parcel of brownfield property.[5] They had trusted a Phase I environmental report provided by their consultant determining that "no recognized environmental conditions" (RECs) existed on the property. In other words, according to this report, there were no significant environmental issues requiring further investigation or remediation.

The due diligence period was set to expire in a couple of weeks, and the company would then be locked into closing.

We took a closer look at the Phase I report, reviewed public records and title work, and then interviewed relevant people and parties to learn more about the property and the transaction. After a few days, it became apparent that there were indeed some significant environmental red flags surrounding the property, and the company needed to get out of the contract.

We challenged the Phase I outfit about the presence of leaking oil and fuel drums, underground storage tanks, fly-ash piles, and an oil-water separator on the property. All of these had been noted but were tucked away near the end of the report and disregarded. We then pushed the outfit to revise the Phase I report to accurately reflect these conditions as RECs. This strategy enabled us to make a strong argument for our client to back out of the agreement and avoid purchasing a property with hazardous environmental conditions.

We terminated the agreement, and afterward we helped our client find a less-risky parcel to set up operations. We then collaborated with them to develop and negotiate the necessary contracts and agreements to facilitate a successful closing.

---

5   Brownfield property is land that has previously been developed for industrial or commercial use and might be contaminated with hazardous waste or pollution—as opposed to greenfield property, which is undeveloped land.

This story is just one example of the way due diligence can protect you from unforeseen dangers before closing a real estate deal. In fact, there are quite a few things you need to look for before you sign on the dotted line, and I've created a helpful list you guide you through them.

Navigating Legal & Regulatory Landscapes

When you're diving into the world of real estate, whether it's your first investment or your fiftieth, understanding the legal and regulatory environment is like having a good map in uncharted territory. Here's how you can navigate this complex landscape:

1. **Understand Local Zoning Laws**: Before anything else, get familiar with local zoning laws. These regulations dictate what can be built where, and more importantly, what can't. A property might look perfect for your commercial venture, but if zoning laws say it's residential only, you're looking at a bureaucratic battle or a change in plans. Always check current zoning, but also look into future zoning plans. Municipalities might have upcoming changes that could affect your investment.

2. **Title Searches and Insurance**: Never skip this step. A title search ensures the property is free from liens or disputes that could haunt you later. Title insurance then protects you from financial loss due to defects in the title that might have been missed. Think of it as your safety net—it's not just about finding problems but also about protecting yourself from the unforeseen ones.

3. **Environmental Assessments**: Remember, what's beneath the surface can be just as crucial as what's on it. Environmental due diligence, including Phase I (initial site review) and possibly Phase II (detailed sampling and testing) assessments, can uncover issues like contamination which not only affect the value but could saddle you with cleanup responsibilities.

This isn't just due diligence—it's about avoiding a potential environmental and financial disaster.

4. **Regulatory Compliance**: Real estate isn't just about location; it's about compliance. From building codes to Americans with Disabilities Act (ADA) requirements, your property needs to comply with a myriad of regulations. Non-compliance can lead to fines, forced renovations, or operational bans. Here, consulting with a legal expert who knows real estate can save you from future legal entanglements.

5. **Engage with Community and Planning Commissions**: Sometimes, the law isn't just written in books—it's spoken in town halls. Engaging with local planning commissions or community boards can give you insights into public sentiment or upcoming changes that aren't yet formalized. This step can be pivotal if your project requires public approval or if you're looking to influence or understand future regulatory shifts.

6. **Contract Negotiation with Legal Insight**: When you're at the negotiation table, having legal counsel ensures that the contract reflects all the due diligence findings. This isn't just about price negotiation; it's about risk allocation. Who's responsible if an underground tank is discovered? What if there's an ancient easement that restricts development? Your contract should answer these questions clearly.

7. **Stay Updated and Agile**: Laws change, and so do regulations. What was compliant last year might not be this year. Subscribing to legal updates, joining real estate networks, or even participating in local government can keep you ahead of changes that could affect your investment.

Remember, in real estate, due diligence isn't just a phase—it's your shield against the unforeseen. Navigating the legal and regulatory landscape requires diligence, foresight, and sometimes, a bit of legal wizardry. With each step, you're not just buying property; you're securing peace of mind.

Leveraging Technology in Real Estate Due Diligence

Modern technology has transformed due diligence in real estate. Drones can now provide aerial views to assess property conditions, boundaries, and even potential environmental issues from above. Geographic Information Systems (GIS) can overlay flood zones, soil types, and other critical data directly onto property maps. Moreover, digital document management systems can organize all your due diligence materials, making them easily accessible and searchable, which is invaluable when dealing with the plethora of documents involved in real estate transactions.

Entitlements

Your ability to effectively run your business on the property after closing may largely depend on the existence of certain federal, state, or local entitlements. An entitlement refers to permissions which are granted to a piece of a property, allowing it to be used in specific ways. For example, some properties may be zoned for residential use, others for commercial use, and so on.

Thus, if you're a product component manufacturer, you may only be able to operate your business within specific areas of the city zoned for industrial use. You wouldn't be able to operate the same business on property zoned for agricultural use.

If you plan to develop the land to build such operations from the ground up, there will invariably be a host of permits and approvals that are required by state and local agencies, which could result in months of applications and meetings prior to any final issuance. Some of those meetings may include public hearings, which give the general public the opportunity to argue for and against your proposed development. You'll probably have to address those concerns, so be prepared.

Many of these entitlements may already be in place, which should make this part of the process a lot easier for you, but you need to find out how long any additional entitlement processes could last. Depending on what you uncover, you may need to incorporate deadline extensions into your purchase agreement.

The Real Estate Checklist

Many of the due diligence items listed below are "contingencies" to a buyer's obligation to close on a purchase, which is a fancy way of saying if they are not met, the buyer has the right to walk away from the deal and get their earnest money back.

With that in mind, here's a list of items to consider:

1) Seller Authorization

First, you need to know upfront who you're purchasing real estate from, especially if it's a corporation, LLC, partnership, or another business entity with multiple owners. Make sure the seller actually exists and is authorized to sell the property. You can do this by requesting and reviewing a resolution from the entity authorizing the sale of the property. This will minimize the likelihood of any post-closing entanglements with potential rogue owners who might come out of the woodwork to claim they didn't consent to the sale. Typically, the title company issuing a policy of title insurance will provide a satisfactory form of resolution.

2) Title Report

You should be able to obtain an updated title report from a reputable title company, which will list all relevant interests touching the property, along with the documents supporting those interests. Review these documents to determine the extent of any interests, encumbrances, or even ownership by third parties in the property. There may be mortgages, deeds of trust, or other liens that have been voluntarily or involuntarily granted (or created) by the seller while owning the property, including judgments against the seller and government liens due to failure to pay taxes. Covenants, conditions, restrictions, easements, and other agreements affecting the property may also exist, any of which could potentially limit (or even prohibit) your particular type of business from operating on that property.

3) Surveys

When most people think of surveys, they think of things like boundary lines, lot sizes, and property descriptions. However, surveys can offer much more, including determining if the property is in a flood zone, as well as a detailed visualization of the specific locations of wetlands, setbacks, utilities, and easements on the parcel. They can also determine if there are any other legal or contractual issues that could potentially affect your occupation of and operation on the property.

Let's say you're looking to purchase a parcel of land to develop a distribution center for your products. An updated survey will help you and your architect create an appropriate footprint design for your building that doesn't violate any of these interests.

4) Verification of Property Use Rights

As discussed earlier, make sure the property has the necessary permissions or can be used for your intended business activities. In addition to your own research, the seller should have documents and information related to property usage that can provide further guidance and assistance. Check for zoning compliance and any required permits or variances that might affect your ability to operate as planned.

Missing entitlements can unravel even the most promising deals. Consider the case of a developer, eager to transform an old industrial site into a modern residential complex in a bustling urban fringe. This developer, let's call him Alex, had a vision that promised both community revitalization and substantial returns. However, in his rush to capitalize on market trends, Alex overlooked a pivotal aspect of due diligence: thorough entitlement checks.

The property in question was zoned for industrial use with a historical preservation tag due to its significance in the city's industrial past. Alex's plan for residential lofts required not just a simple rezoning but a complex entitlement process involving public hearings, historical review boards, and a series of permits. This oversight came to light only after initial demolition had begun, halting the project indefinitely. The implications were manifold: investor confidence waned, legal fees piled up, and the community's reaction was mixed, with some seeing it as a missed opportunity for new housing while others appreciated the preservation of industrial heritage.

Alex was forced into a reactive stance, engaging deeply with community stakeholders and historians to modify his plans. He proposed a design that integrated elements of the factory's history, turning the project into a living museum of sorts. This adaptation, while innovative, came at a significantly higher cost and extended timeline. The ordeal taught a harsh lesson on the importance of comprehensive due diligence, particularly in understanding and securing all necessary entitlements before breaking ground.

This case underscores the intricate dance of development, where the rhythm is often set by regulatory entitlements. Missing a step in this dance, like failing to secure the right entitlements, not only delays projects but can transform potential success stories into cautionary tales of oversight. Alex's experience serves as a reminder that in real estate, vision must be matched with meticulous preparation, especially in the legal and communal landscapes where projects are built.

5) Environmental Reports

Another important due diligence step is determining if there are any issues with the soil or groundwater, as we learned in the earlier case study. If you're purchasing undeveloped greenfield property with no prior industrial or commercial use, this shouldn't be much of a concern. On the other hand, if you're purchasing brownfield property that has had significant prior industrial use, you'll want to obtain all existing environmental assessments and reports to fully understand the potential hazards that may exist.

If there are no such reports, consider engaging a reputable inspector to conduct a Phase I environmental site assessment to determine the existence of any RECs (e.g., underground storage tanks). If the Phase I assessment discovers that the property may contain hazardous substances, then you may need to take it to the next level by having a Phase II assessment performed to physically assess the soil and groundwater for the presence of contaminants.

6) Leases

Sometimes, tenants or landlords will have a recorded memorandum of lease in the public property records—in which case, a title report will inform you of the lease's existence. However, most of the time, the existence of a lease isn't public information. Either way, it's imperative that you find out if a third-party tenant has the right to possess the property according to the lease. Otherwise, you may be in for a costly surprise when you purchase the property and discover that a tenant has a ten-year lease.

Many states have pro-tenant eviction statutes that make it very hard, if not impossible, to get rid of an unwanted tenant with a legally valid lease. For that reason, it's always better to address tenant issues proactively with your seller before you sign a purchase agreement, and certainly before you close on the property.

If the seller is representing to you that there are no tenants, then the purchase agreement should specifically include a statement from the seller that says they have not leased or sold the property to a third party, and no third parties are in possession of the property. Typically, you'll be able to tour the property in person prior to closing, at which time you can visually observe whether anyone other than the seller seems to be using the property.

Now, if the property already has tenants and you're still considering buying it, then you should research local rent-control laws and require the tenant to provide a tenant estoppel certificate. This certificate will confirm the existing lease terms and conditions, including the amount of rent, duration of the lease, whether the lease is in good standing (or if there are existing defaults by either party), and any modifications or amendments to the original lease. This certificate will also confirm the obligations of the property owner—which is about to be you!

7) Pending or Threatened Actions

Finding out after purchase that you've inherited tenants is bad enough, but you could also inherit any pending or threatened claims, lawsuits, or other actions involving the property. These may not appear on a title search, so you'll want to proactively ask about them.

Pending actions come in many forms, including:

- Notices of default by the seller's bank

- A letter from a contractor to the seller demanding payment for work done on the property

- A letter from a state notifying the seller that they will be taking some of the property by eminent domain proceedings to expand a highway

- An agency notice regarding discharge of hazardous materials at the property

In the purchase agreement, insist that the seller provide you copies of every letter, notice, demand, or lawsuit that in any way involves some potential action against the real estate you're purchasing. That way you can meaningfully evaluate the significance of each one.

THE LEGAL WELLNESS KIT

8) Contracts & Utilities

If you're purchasing property that has an existing structure on it, you'll want to obtain copies of all agreements or contracts with any vendors servicing the property for the seller. That way you can determine if you'll inherit any ongoing obligations.

If you're purchasing undeveloped land, you might discover that there are no utilities nearby. If that's the case, then your analysis should include an exploration of whether or not the nearest municipality is willing to extend utility services to the property and what your additional costs would be for doing so.

You'll also want to obtain copies of any insurance policies affecting the property, so you'll understand any risk-transfer issues, including enhanced or reduced coverage or premium costs. In geographic areas experiencing an increasing number of adverse weather events, such as hurricanes and wildfires, some properties may no longer be insurable because several major insurance companies have stopped doing business in those areas. Though it's not necessary, you may consider adding a contingency that says you must be able to obtain satisfactory insurance on the property before you're obligated to close on the sale.

9) Physical Inspection

Finally, conduct a thorough physical inspection of the property to determine the extent of any deferred maintenance and immediate repairs or replacements that will need to be made. The purchase agreement should require the seller to provide all records of service and repairs to the property. Your physical inspection should also look for any code noncompliance, including local fire and life safety requirements and federal laws like the ADA.

Once due diligence uncovers issues, how you negotiate can significantly affect the outcome of your real estate deal. If environmental issues or title complications arise, you might negotiate for a price reduction, request the seller to remedy the issue before purchase, or include specific contingencies in the contract. A sidebar or section on negotiation tactics, like using findings to adjust escrow amounts or to extend due diligence periods for further investigation, can equip buyers with the tools to turn due diligence insights into tangible benefits.

Due diligence isn't just about assessing the present state of a property but also forecasting its future viability. Consider factors like climate change, which might affect sea levels or weather patterns, thereby impacting property locations. Look into upcoming zoning changes or infrastructure projects nearby that could either enhance or diminish property value.

A forward-thinking approach in due diligence can safeguard your investment against future uncertainties, ensuring that today's wise purchase doesn't become tomorrow's regret.

THAT'S A LOT OF PAPERWORK!

I've just given you a rather long list of items you need to look for during your due diligence *before* you close on a prospective business or real estate acquisition deal. Your seller might balk at the scope and length of your due diligence process. To avoid this, I recommend having a letter of intent in place that contains agreed-upon terms to be incorporated into the final purchase agreement.

A letter of intent is a document (typically non-binding) which is prepared by one of the parties (typically the seller, and signed by the buyer) outlining the key terms that will form the basis of the agreement. For example:

- A list of the assets that are going to be purchased

- The purchase price itself, as well as any downpayment, amount due at closing, financing, etc.

- A general outline of the due diligence the prospective buyer will conduct, and the timeframe for completion after the agreement is signed

- Employment arrangements for existing employees of the seller (if any)

- Exclusivity (i.e., whether the seller may approach other prospective buyers while the parties are under agreement) and if so, for how long

- Confidentiality if the parties want to keep their prospective purchase and sale under wraps

- The jurisdiction and venue where any legal proceedings would need to commence in the event of a dispute between the parties regarding the letter of intent, and ultimately the final agreement itself

- How long the letter of intent will last, as well as under what circumstances it may be terminated

- Which party will be responsible for preparing the initial draft of the final agreement (keeping in mind the discussion about one-sided contracts in Chapter 2)

These terms will ultimately be preserved in a much more robust purchase and sale agreement, but It's important to document the principal items agreed-upon by the parties to minimize confusion during the agreement drafting process.

OPEN YOUR EYES, LOOK WITHIN

Due diligence isn't only necessary in business mergers, acquisitions, and real estate sales—it can also provide a framework for maintaining your ongoing business and legal health to ensure long-term success and stability. And regular due diligence will help to ensure that your business remains attractive to prospective buyers should you decide to sell your company to pursue other interests.

It's just like scheduling regular checkups with the doctor in Preventive Medicine. Conduct regular self-exams, sometimes called a "review of business systems," to clarify your current business and legal health and find targeted opportunities for improvement. In doing so, you'll avoid potential risk exposures before they start to grow and multiply.

Here's what a business self-exam might look like:

- Review your existing business entities to ensure ongoing alignment with tax strategies and tax opportunities, as well as to mitigate legal and business risks.

- Review all business formalities conducted during the year to ensure legal compliance, as well as accurate and appropriate business storytelling through minutes, consents, and resolutions.

- Review your existing and prospective geographical presence to ensure appropriate state-based registrations.

- Review your existing and prospective license, permit, and regulatory registration requirements to ensure ongoing compliance.

- Review your contract practices to ensure proactive negotiation and development practices are being followed, and that business counterparts are compliant with quality and safety standards, insurance levels, or other contractual requirements.

- Review your business continuity practices to ensure there isn't an overreliance on a key supplier or vendor that could result in a business interruption.

- Review your legal, regulatory, and contractual compliance programs to ensure appropriate training and documetation is taking place.

- Review your insurance program to ensure risk transfer practices align with existing enterprise-wide exposures, and that vague or ambiguous language is addressed and clarified before claims arise.

- Review any potential claims *against* third parties, as well as claims *by* third parties, that could be tendered to an insurance carrier.

- Review all existing claims and lawsuits to ensure litigation strategies are business-forward.

Conducting ongoing business self-exams like this will pay off big time if you end up selling your business or real estate. If you receive a detailed due diligence request from a buyer, you'll be able to quickly and efficiently provide all requested documents and disclose any potential troublesome issues.

To be clear, you don't have to disclose *all* information about your business or real estate during a due diligence process, but failing to disclose any objectively important issue before closing the sale could derail the whole thing, or force you to sell at a substantially reduced price. If that happens, you also get to enjoy diminished credibility in the marketplace if you attempt to sell it again. Additionally, failing to disclose any major issues could open you up to fraud allegations and even litigation to undo the sale.

Since you'll probably have to disclose *some* confidential or proprietary information about your business—which may include key inventions, trade secrets, customers, contracts, and employees—make sure you have a mutually acceptable NDA in place prior to sharing. Remember, there is no guarantee that this transaction will close, so if you fail to adequately protect your confidential materials prior to disclosing them, you may end up arming a prospective purchaser with enough know-how to become a competitor. If that happens, you'll have to spend a whole lot of money in litigation to stop them.

Ultimately, due diligence should be a standard component of every significant business transaction. Not only should you peek under the hood of any target business or real estate parcel to make sure you're not buying a lemon, but you should also regularly peek under the hood of your own business to make sure it's consistently operating at optimal health!

Due Diligence Checklist

____ Always conduct an in-depth review, analysis, and evaluation of any target business or real estate prior to closing to make sure there are no red flags that might come back to bite you.

____ During due diligence, you will likely need to negotiate and sign an NDA.

____ Navigate the legal and regulatory landscapes affecting the real estate acquisition:

    ____ Understand local zoning laws applicable to your investment.

    ____ Conduct a title search on the property and obtain title insurance.

    ____ Assess environmental issues affecting the property.

    ____ Engage with community and planning commissions if necessary.

    ____ Stay up to speed on laws and regulations, and leverage available technology.

____ Consider utilizing legal counsel in contract negotiations and to assist with the due diligence and closing process.

continued...

___ Request the following documents from the seller: seller authorization, title report, surveys, verifications of usage, environmental reports, leases, pending or threatened actions, contracts, and utilities—and be sure to conduct a physical inspection of the property.

___ Utilizing due diligence frameworks, conduct regular self-exams for your own business and legal health as well.

SAFEGUARDING YOUR BUSINESS'S HEALTH

Just as you wouldn't ignore a persistent cough or a strange ache, you shouldn't overlook your business's health. At the beginning of this book, we drew parallels between Preventive Medicine and Preventive Law. Both disciplines aim to protect, promote, and maintain well-being. Throughout this book, we've explored how to apply this philosophy to your business, ensuring it not only survives but thrives.

Remember the coffee shop owner entangled in a supply contract dispute? That scenario underscored the essence of what we've discussed: proactive legal health checks can prevent small issues from becoming catastrophic business conditions. Just as a physician con-ducts a comprehensive review of systems to catch health problems early, your business requires a similar approach to its legal and operational frameworks.

By now, you understand that:

1. **Business Formation & Governance** are your business's foundational health, akin to a strong immune system, setting the stage for robust growth and legal protection.

2. **Contract Negotiation & Development** acts like your business's diagnostic tools, helping you to foresee and mitigate risks before they manifest into complications.

3. **Compliance Policies & Training** serve as your business's daily health regimen, keeping operations fit and within legal boundaries.

4. **Employment Practices** are the heart of your business, pumping vitality through your operations when managed with care and legality.

5. **Insurance** is your safety net, there to catch you when unforeseen events occur, much like health insurance for unexpected medical issues.

6. **Managing Claims & Lawsuits** is your strategic response to symptoms, ensuring that when legal ailments arise, they're treated effectively without compromising the business's health.

7. **Due Diligence** in business or real estate deals is your full-body scan, ensuring no hidden issues exist when introducing outside elements into your ecosystem.

Adopting these principles of Preventive Law means you're not just reacting to legal ailments—you're actively engaging in practices that foster a healthy, resilient business. You're not merely dodging legal pitfalls; rather, you're building a business with foresight, equipped to navigate the complexities of today's market with confidence.

As you close this book, remember it's not meant to gather dust on a shelf. Let it be your ongoing reference, your manual for maintaining the legal health of your business. Whether you're facing a new contract, a potential lawsuit, or expanding your operations, revisit these pages and let it be your ongoing reference manual:

- Eyeing a new business acquisition? Flip back to the due diligence chapter.

- Hit with a lawsuit? Refresh yourself on managing claims.

- Puzzled over an insurance claim? Revisit that insurance section.

In essence, Preventive Law isn't just about avoiding legal diseases; it's about creating an environment where your business can flourish, where legal wellness contributes to your overall success. By integrating these practices, you ensure your business doesn't just endure; it excels, prepared for whatever legal or operational challenges come its way—just like a well-maintained body is ready for life's physical demands.

As you move forward, I challenge you to review your current business practices through the lens of Preventive Law. Implement these strategies not just as a defense mechanism but as a core part of your business's growth strategy. By mastering Preventive Law, you're not just safeguarding your business; you're setting a new standard for leadership in your industry. Let's make proactive legal health the new norm!

ABOUT THE AUTHOR

Chris Keefer is a legal strategist, business consultant, and entrepreneur recognized for his role in helping businesses incorporate Preventive Law into their decision-making. With an extensive background in both legal practice and business and risk management, Keefer offers clients a unique blend of strategic legal advice and business foresight, enabling them to confidently navigate the complexities of the corporate landscape.

Over the course of more than 25 years in practice, Keefer has held significant roles where he's applied his legal expertise to address real-world business challenges. His comprehensive experience includes positions such as in-house counsel for multiple ten-figure product manufacturers, strategic advisor for both publicly-traded and privately-held global corporations, and Professor at the University of Notre Dame Law School. This rich background infuses his work with profound insights into diverse business settings.

Keefer's approach to Preventive Law isn't just about avoiding legal pitfalls; it's about empowering businesses to make proactive decisions that support their strategic goals. He transcends traditional legal counsel by helping them anticipate and manage legal and business risks effectively.

An active writer and speaker, Keefer shares his knowledge on strategic legal planning, risk management, and compliance through various publications and presentations at national conferences. His method, combining legal strategy with business acumen, prepares companies for success in an increasingly intricate legal landscape.

www.ingramcontent.com/pod-product-compliance
Lightning Source LLC
Chambersburg PA
CBHW031850200326
41597CB00012B/345